CW00741177

LIFE'S A BITCH, THEN YOU TRY

Finding significance through gratitude, connection and simplicity

Danny McAllister

Life's a Bitch, then You Try
Finding significance through gratitude, connection and simplicity

First published in Australia by McAllister's Fitness Pty Ltd 2021
www.mcallistersfitness.com.au

 A catalogue record for this
book is available from the
National Library of Australia

ISBN: 978-0-6450519-0-2 (pbk)

Typesetting and design by Publicious Book Publishing
Published in collaboration with Publicious Book Publishing
www.publicious.com.au

DEDICATION

To Mum and Dad thank you for the sacrifices you made to give us the life we have. (I still miss you both and think of you every day). To my brothers who all in their own way have taught me how to navigate life. Growing up in a large family was, at times pretty tough yet we always found a way to pull through and make life fun. It's somewhere only we know!!

CONTENTS

**Chapter 6: Simplicity, Mindset
and Having Fun**

Conclusion

Acknowledgements

Although writing this book has been a lot of hard work it's also been heaps of fun. It wouldn't have happened if it wasn't for the support, encouragement and belief that my family and friends have given me to see it come to fruition. I want to thank the following people for helping me with writing this book.

My beautiful wife Anndrea – Thank you for all your love and understanding, it's never ending. There were times when I struggled to write and you encouraged me to continue, you have traveled this writing journey with me, as a sounding board, a support crew and my genius. You are amazing.

Lorraine Spiteri – Thank you for all your hard work and effort in editing this book. Your attention to detail and grammar are second to none. I know it must have been quite the challenge turning my wordy babble into a structured and easy read whilst still allowing my voice to be heard in the words, and for that I'm truly grateful.

To everyone who has helped me navigate life up till now. From those who have supported me and shared their wisdom to help me grow, to those who have shown me what I don't want to be. For all the good and bad I've encountered on this journey they call life, thank you all for the learning.

Introduction

Ever had the feeling of anxiety after you've set yourself some success goals? Don't worry it happens and a lot. I used to be a prolific goal setter and success planner and had what I considered a wonderful process in doing so. I would sit down for hours working out a plan for all aspects of my life. I'd get all excited about what I was venturing into and how success would look for me only to become anxious and overwhelmed by the daunting task of what lay ahead. How was it I'd get anxious about something that got me excited?? It took me years of frustration, disappointment and feeling like a failure to realise that the pressure I put on myself to achieve success was actually making me feel unsuccessful.

From experience, I've discovered that for the multi-million dollar business the self-help industry is, the success rate doesn't seem to be that impressive. There appears to be a massive percentage of the population who actually struggle with anxiety, stress and being overwhelmed by what I believe is the perceived pressure to achieve, be better or successful. So if the self-help industry is thriving, why then is mental health, sadness and anxiety so prevalent?

Don't get me wrong I'm definitely not against the self-help industry and yes I still love to read books that will help me grow and become a better person. Saying that, with all the mountains of books I've read, seminars I've attended and podcasts, videos etc I've listened too and watched, I've also come to realise that although they tell me the story that I can achieve success I struggle to free myself from the guilt, shame and uncertainty of what not achieving my goals and being unsuccessful does to my self-esteem.

Apparently the number one goal most people desire in life is – Happiness, how's that working out so far?

The truth is, we'd all like to be happier, more confident, smarter, financial, mentally and physically stronger, slimmer, fitter, better, right! I don't think there's too many people who would say nah, don't need that crap I don't mind being shit. Yet when it comes to the doing and making that happen we tend to struggle. I remember when I first started working in the Health and Fitness industry, I wanted to be the best!! I spent hundreds of dollars and hours absorbing anything I could get my hands on to find the winning formula that would bring me success. I was constantly chasing the next big thing trying to achieve the euphoric high that success would bring and in hindsight that pursuit became pressure rather than enjoyment. There were successes in that journey, but sadly for a long time I never really stopped to celebrate or appreciate them due to the constant battle in my head believing that success will bring me happiness and make my life complete.

What's wrong with that you might ask?

I've looked at success from many perspectives now and have come to the conclusion that success is different for everyone. Success is a personal thing and how to go about it is purely up to the individual. To some it's appears to come easily while for others the pressure surrounding it can be a daunting and overwhelming. Success is often sold as the pathway to happiness and through attaining it therein lies the prize. I wish this was true but from experience and research I don't believe this is so. In fact, there are many highly successful people who are miserable, to the point of suffering depression and suicidal thoughts. So you could say success has a darker side, it can produce feelings of inadequacy, shame, isolation, pressure, anxiety and failure. I think these feelings come from the guilt and fear of missing out tactics used by social media and the self-help industry to motivate action. Success is sold as this tangible thing that brings happiness, confidence, financial stability, prestige or status. I think too often when success is promoted this way it can do more harm than good. Sadly you can have all of those things yet still feel unhappy, inadequate, disconnected or a failure and I've experienced this phenomenon and have struggled with why my successes weren't bringing me happiness. This took me a long time to understand and that is where I became interested in the pursuit of significance as opposed to the pursuit of success.

Don't get me wrong this isn't a hate on success, the self-help industry, social media or about stopping anyone from ever pursuing success, it's about doing your best with what you have to find the significance in what you do. It's about working out what inspires you to continually improve, learn and achieve without the unnecessary guilt and pressures we often put on ourselves to achieve it. Which brings me to the reason why I wrote this book.

The idea behind this book is to get you inspired about you, to get you to use your potential to the very best and to help you find significance in whatever you choose to do. I want people to understand you don't have to be extraordinary to do amazing things, when you eliminate some of the unnecessary pressures and anxiety we put on ourselves to be successful. I want you to help make the world a better place through building meaningful relationships, connecting with others and reducing the anxiety and sadness around trying to be perfect.

Throughout the book I will share my thoughts, stories and reasons why I believe finding significance in what you do is not only gratifying but a healthier approach to life than the pursuit of success. I will cover the things that can help bring us closer to creating a meaningful life. Why stress and anxiety are so prevalent when pursuing success and how to reduce it. And why focusing on what's important to you while having fun is vital in designing you.

I hope this book inspires you to go on a self-discovery journey that helps you be happy in your skin and gain a better understanding of what you really want from life. I believe the pressure that surrounds success today is overwhelming and is a contributing factor restricting people from experiencing life and exploring their potential. Sometimes we need to step away from the busy-ness and distractions of life to find the purpose behind it. When we can be comfortable in our skin and understand the significance of why, that's success!!

Tread your own path!

CHAPTER 1:
Significance and Success

Significance

As a kid growing up in a little country town, I always felt the pressure of being accepted or having to be good at something to fit in. As much as I didn't mind a little competition, the fear of failure, or not being good enough was huge and there was always someone to let you know when you did fail. Some might say that's life and if you can't handle it, too bad. Although at times that might be true, you shouldn't have to be fearful, anxious or worried about whether your success allows you to fit in. This kind of thinking creates a comparison mentality where we tend to measure ourselves or our success by comparing ourselves to others, which often creates pressure, insecurity, doubt, anxiety, and a fear of failure.

We somehow need to move away from the 'success equals acceptance' mentality and look at it in a different way. I'm not saying there shouldn't be any competition or winners and losers but if we're constantly comparing ourselves to others as our motivational tool to be good enough, we'll be constantly setting ourselves up for disappointment. No matter how amazing your life is, for some silly reason we often see the grass as greener somewhere else and, in the process, let our insecurities restrict us from taking chances.

For example, instead of using someone else's success as a measuring stick for ours, we need to be realistic and honest about our abilities and what we seriously can accomplish. By being realistic about what you can accomplish within your capabilities, you reduce the pressure and anxiety associated with the comparison model. The thing is to never put a limit on your potential but to know your capabilities. This sets a standard where your chance of succeeding increases without the added pressure. The satisfaction of knowing you gave your best and did everything within the limits of your ability is, by the way, success. It's by keeping your expectations real and not setting your benchmark for success too high, or based on someone else's success, that you don't become overwhelmed.

Having realistic expectations and focusing on finding meaning for what you do increases your self-belief and chance of success. When you place value in what you do and are truly comfortable in your skin, you're well on the path to finding significance.

What is significance?

The dictionary meaning of significance is: *The quality of being worthy of attention, importance, special, unique or needed.*

We all want to feel liked, needed, important, or special in some way, right? It gives us a sense of self-worth and purpose. Significance can have many meanings depending on the individual but for me, significance is:

- Living life aligned with my values.
- Living life with a meaning and purpose that allows me to be/do better.
- Knowing that I am constantly adding value to other people's lives as well as mine.
- Knowing that who I am, what I stand for and believe in, helps make my part of the world a better place.
- To love and be connected to those who are important to me.
- Having the self-awareness to realise my faults and failures are just as important as my successes.
- Having situational awareness to know what's going on around me and be more present.
- Having an internal energy that inspires me to keep learning and growing as a person so I can leave a legacy that inspires others to be their best.

There are many amazing people who have left a legacy that has made the world a better place because they found significance in what they do. People like Nelson Mandela for his fight against apartheid, Martin Luther King for his fight against racism, Mother Teresa for her dedication to helping the poor, and Mahatma Gandhi for his non-violent movement for Indian independence. These are examples of massive legacies that changed the world forever. The point is that they all found significance in what they believed in. I'm not suggesting we all have to produce amazing results like these inspirational human beings but, by finding significance in what you do, although it may not be world changing, it may be enough to change the piece of the world that you inhabit.

How good would that feel?

Have you ever been in a situation where someone has given you a compliment or praised you for what you've done? It's nice to be valued, right? Being valued for who you are and how you act is success based on significance. Too often we disregard these moments because we think they're insignificant or don't make an impact on our world. The sooner we move away from the thinking that success needs to be something major and replace this idea with doing little things of significance, the greater the chances are of actually achieving measurable success. The 'success equals doing major things' mindset can be overwhelming and can often create pressure and anxiety around achievements and performance. So instead of being excited about pursuing a goal, we become daunted and overwhelmed by the prospect of what lies ahead. This leads to us tending to make excuses for why our idea won't work or make a difference.

Significance is about focusing on the small things that produce better outcomes. It's about doing the things that have meaning and give you the purpose to continue doing what you do. When we understand the meaning of what we do, we feel more in control and aligned with our values, and this helps keep us enthused and on track. Whereas, although we are enthused sometimes in the pursuit of success, we can let our fears get in the way. We restrict ourselves due to our fear of failure, uncertainty, rejection, change, being judged, inadequacy: the list goes on! This can stop us from taking a chance.

I remember when I first started as a personal trainer. I was working in a commercial gym and decided it was time to move on and open my own gym. There were plenty of reasons to do it: the space I was occupying was too small, the gym culture and environment wasn't aligned with mine and my business was definitely big enough to make the move. I definitely had enough incentive to leave but, due to my fears, I kept putting it off. I would tell myself stories about why it wasn't the right time. The excuses flowed: the economy is weak and it's too risky, I don't have the finance, my business knowledge is poor, I need to learn more, my practical skills and experience aren't good enough to go it alone, and the biggest one: what if I fail? I was constantly justifying why it wasn't a good idea and why it wasn't a good time to take the plunge. In hindsight, all I was doing was procrastinating. Why? Because I was afraid, and the prospect of failing was daunting. At the time, my mentor questioned my hesitation. He said there will never be a right time and making excuses is fear and what you're doing is letting your fears hold you back.

Success

I had to confront my fears and focus on why I wanted this. It wasn't easy but the move was a lot easier than I thought it would be. I definitely wasn't an overnight sensation, but my eyes were opened to what was possible. With that, my confidence began to grow. Like the Paul Kelly song *'From Little Things Big Things Grow'*, over time, I gradually built the business up which allowed me to grow and move towards my potential. It's moments like these when focusing on what's important and doing the little things, that the path of significance appears. On reflection, this experience was a great example of how the pressure I placed on myself around success caused overthinking, stress and anxiety.

What is success?

Success, according to the dictionary, is:

- The achievement of something that you have been trying to do.
- Someone or something that achieves a high position in a particular field, makes a lot of money, or is admired a great deal.
- Attaining wealth, prosperity and/or fame.

Success, like significance, is also about having purpose, being important or needed. Sadly though, I believe the concept of success is promoted somewhat differently to significance. Success tends to be focused more on extrinsic rewards like fame, fortune, financial gains, status, title, and material things that supposedly bring you happiness.

Success gets marketed as this tangible thing that, if you work hard and follow the steps, it will come to you. If it was that simple, I think we'd all be successful but, what they don't tell you is that success requires more than effort and following the steps. It requires us to be able to manage our fears, faults and insecurities which, most of the time, are the biggest difficulties.

Somehow success has become a product being sold by people hoping to make a buck out of their so-called 'success secret'. The amount of people selling their 'How to be a success' products is extraordinary and sadly, the money they make far outweighs the success rate of the buyer. The thing is, success doesn't just happen because you attended a workshop or bought a product. It requires more than following someone else's path. A system, procedure or a workshop may point you in the right direction, but it isn't necessarily an automatic pathway to success.

Unfortunately, due to the influence of the Internet and social media today, success has become a platform for people to brag about their obtained wealth, fortune, prestige, status, or fame. Look on any social media platform and you'll see someone banging on about their story of their rags to riches journey, backed up with pictures of them now living the dream. By the way, there are some great stories in this space but, just because someone tells a compelling story, has a flash car or big house, it doesn't necessarily equate to success or happiness.

Obtaining success

Back when I started my business, I would read as much as I could get my hands on about success and how to achieve it. I was inspired and motivated to go where others had gone and, hopefully in the process, experience the same too. The thought of what success would bring was exciting, so I never really questioned how it was associated with happiness. I bought the dream that success brings happiness. Why wouldn't I want a piece of that? Over the years of pursuing this dream, I began to realise, as I achieved a level of success, that the goal at the time would be superseded by the quest for something bigger or better. My successes never seemed to make me happy. I was forever chasing the next big thing. Chasing success became a game that never seemed to end. I was always looking for more and, depending on what I was reading or who I was listening to at the time, my journey was affected by the comparison and I would become disappointed.

I was constantly comparing my success and happiness to someone else's. This type of behaviour was unhealthy and caused me anxiety. I would either get disappointed with my considered lack of progress or become jealous of someone else's. I started to undermine my self-worth. I felt I was never good enough, so my focus quickly turned to comparing myself to others instead of being proud of what I had done.

I realised I needed to rethink this approach. It was based too much on comparisons and following someone else's version of success. This not only impeded my progress but stopped me from doing the things that resonated with me, the things that brought me joy or were significant to me.

Why pursue significance over success?

Quite often we have goals, ambitions or desires that we think align with our values but instead, seem to be set to feed our ego. We sometimes sacrifice our values in the pursuit of success, believing that success and our values are aligned and then we wonder why we struggle to find the significance in what we do. We need to move away from the ideology of 'with success comes significance and happiness' to the ideology of finding significance first and realising that success specifically for us then follows.

Significance is driven by your personal values and cannot be purchased. It's about creating a life where you explore your potential and, hopefully, grow to become a better person. It's about building an environment that's positive, more appreciative and inspires others to do the same.

When you align your values with what you do, things just flow. Your path seems clearer. You get enthused about what you're doing and become grateful for the opportunities you encounter. On the other hand, pursuit of success has become more about prestige, the judgement of others and status which, regrettably for some, causes fear and anxiety due to the perceived pressures placed around it. Pursuing success should be something we feel good about, not something we fear.

Just as success must be defined to be achieved, so must significance. While both require some form of sacrifice, success can sometimes come at the expense of your values. If your goals aren't aligned with your values, you may find you lose enthusiasm quickly because they don't resonate, therefore your heart isn't truly in it.

In my line of work, I'm consistently talking to people about goals and the pursuit of success. Frequently I've heard someone talk about how good they'll feel and how happy life will be once they reach their goal. What I find interesting is watching these people start off so enthusiastically and then, because of a setback or hurdle, they soon lose the drive to continue. They definitely had the motivation to get started but somehow lacked the drive to keep going. Why? Because most times their goal wasn't aligned with their values.

Too often we set goals based on comparing ourselves to someone else's success. When the focus centres around the extrinsic, it's harder to stay enthused. I remember having a business coach to help me grow my business, which worked well for a while. My business was expanding and my reputation was increasing. So, you could say I was on the path to success. The problem was the more my business grew, the more detached I became from it. My heart wasn't in it and, although things looked good on the outside, they definitely weren't on the inside. The path I was following was being designed by someone else. It was their idea of what they wanted me to be and it didn't align with my values.

As the owner of the business with administrative staff and a team of trainers, I had lost interest and wasn't sure about what I wanted to do. I felt pressured to measure up to the expectations of someone else's version of success and I felt like a failure. I was meant to be the leader, the person full of enthusiasm, inspiring the team, but all I was feeling was pressure and anxiety.

It was hard to be motivated about something that didn't resonate with me or had little meaning. Something had to change. I decided to step away from the noise and mind clutter to spend some time reassessing my goals. I needed to work out what I really wanted, to find meaning in what I did. I was so caught up in the doing that I'd lost touch with my original goal and desperately needed to reconnect with them. Sometimes we can get so swept up in the busyness of life that we end up in a place where we really don't want to be.

This process took a bit of time to sort out but once I reconnected with my why and it aligned with my values, it gave me significance. I now had genuine skin in the game. I had more control and an incentive to keep me going. Too often we chase success in the hope it brings significance whereas if we find the significance first, the chances of success happening increases.

CHAPTER 2:
Expectations

We live in a world full of information, influence and opinion telling us how to be happy, successful, and how to live life to the fullest. The Internet is full of gurus and experts all claiming to have the secret to success and happiness and if you follow their plan, it can be yours too.

There's so much pressure these days to be successful, whether it be in business, financially, vocationally, spiritually, personally, through parenting, family, education, sport, happiness... yet, somehow, if you're not achieving, you're either not trying hard enough or you're a failure. These pressures come from all walks of life: our parents, partners, friends, employers, peers, teachers, schools, coaches, print media, and social media. It's endless. We're constantly being told, 'Believe in yourself, dream big, follow your passion, find something you're good at and pursue it because *you can be anything.*' This, of course, is said with good intentions but what if it doesn't work out? Are you then a failure?

Telling someone they can be anything they want to be is not only wrong, it also places a lot of pressure on the individual to live up to it. The reality is, if you can't sing, the chances of making a career from singing are going to be pretty slim. We need to stop this false motivational pressure because it only leads to disappointment. To think just because you're passionate or good at something you will be successful at it and you'll be happy, is being delusional. Success definitely needs belief, but it also requires a willingness to step out of your comfort zone, work hard, and be committed.

Bizarrely, the pressure and expectations that success comes easily and will bring you happiness has become a major cause of anxiety and sadness. We're sold the story that success, once achieved, brings you happiness. We have gurus sprouting their pearls of wisdom on how they have the formula or steps to success. The multibillion-dollar self-development space is full of these people. Just Google the word *success* and you'll find literally millions of books, workshops, seminars, podcasts, blogs, social media influencers, etc all sprouting their version of how they can help you find success. How often have you heard someone say that by following their steps to success you can have whatever you want? This is fine if it gets you started but no key, secret or formula will keep you motivated long enough to see it through if it doesn't resonate with you or align with your values.

Too often we get caught up in the thought of what success can bring. We follow someone else's version of it and then wonder why we seldom achieve it. When I first started my business, I read so many books on success and how to achieve it. They were great motivation which got me excited about all the possibilities of what I could achieve. I started with great enthusiasm, putting all that theory into practice, and I was feeling excited about what I thought I could achieve. After a while, when things weren't moving as quickly as I hoped, my excitement started to wane, and the application of the theory started to become so much harder. I discovered the theory, although motivational, didn't necessarily mould into the practical. I was now facing the reality that I had to be accountable, so my effort determined my outcome. The dream of possibility and success had now shrunk somewhat. The fun and excitement was getting less and my anxiety and expectations were rising.

I knew the possibilities were still there but the reality of what I needed to do and what lay ahead was quite daunting. I needed to work out what my version of success was and, sadly, with lots of angst, this took some time to find. As much as the pursuit of success was exciting for me, it was also overwhelming and for many years I struggled with the idea of what I thought success had to be and what I really wanted. After many years of trial and many errors, I realised I was following someone else's version of success, which didn't resonate with me nor have any real significance to me. Even though I'd started to achieve some success and validation, it gave minimal joy and left me feeling empty. It's a strange feeling when you're achieving or doing well yet it doesn't resonate. I couldn't connect with the goals I was pursuing, and it concerned me.

Unnecessary pressure to perform or be

Success is marketed as this wonderful thing that, if you believe it, it will happen. You definitely have to believe in what you are aiming to achieve but there's a lot of hard work in there too and the problem is most people want success without the hard work. It would be fantastic if just a thought brought success. Unfortunately, sometimes even when you've put in the work, it still may not happen. In fact, there are no guarantees when it comes to success and although you may have done all the work, followed all the steps and have the belief to succeed, you still may not be that successful.

The truth be known, most of us will only achieve an average amount of success. We'll probably work in an average job, earn an average income, live in an average house, drive an average car, live an average existence and experience an average amount of happiness. Most of us are destined to be average and realistically we should be happy with that, but we live in a world that tells us a different story. We're told we can be anything if we believe it and that we should strive for that but when it doesn't happen, we're made feel as if we're not good enough. This type of thinking creates unnecessary pressure around performance and if you don't meet the so-called expectations, you get disappointed and start to believe the 'we're not good enough' story. The 'believe it and it'll happen' approach is leading people into a false hope that is anything but motivational. In fact, it can be deflating and cause discontentment with our lot in life to the point that we don't feel grateful about the good things we've done and who we are.

By the way, being average is OK and we should be well pleased with it, but we're sold the story that we need to be better. When that doesn't happen, we see ourselves as a failure. Somehow being average is perceived as falling short because it's perceived as a lack of achievement. If we stop the shaming and bullshit hype around success, and accept that being average is OK, we would most likely be so much happier. It's about finding significance in what you do and appreciating that life can be amazing when you align with your values.

As mentioned, often we set our goals based on someone else's version of success and, in doing so, base our goals on comparing ourselves to others. We live in a comparison culture, we compare our life to someone else's and think, 'Why can't I be, do or have the same?' This culture or thinking is nothing new. It's always been a part of being human but has increased over the last decade due to the influence of media. Comparison, at times, can be a good thing, especially when used as an incentive to challenge yourself to do more. I think it's quite healthy to have a little bit of competitiveness in us. It says you have pride and believe in yourself enough to want to be better. The problem arises when the comparison becomes obsessive and makes you want to be like someone else. It's OK to have someone to aspire to but if that comparison creates anxiety and sadness due to what you perceive as your lack of success, then it's unhealthy.

Social media platforms are full of people depicting their life as amazing. They promote their story as this journey full of excitement and fun where wonderful things happen. And when we see their posts, we feel disappointed and wonder why we can't be, or have, the same. We believe that what we're seeing is the truth and compare their success to ours instead of trying to find what works for us. This type of behaviour can be damaging to our self-worth because we feel our world is boring, therefore we aren't as good as the people depicted. We become more about external appearances and we believe things will make us happy rather than working on what resonates with us. It's easy to fall into the trap of thinking that external things will make you happier. It may in the short term but if you can't be happy in your own skin, you'll most probably always see the grass appearing greener on the other side.

Happy in your skin

How many of us can say with absolute confidence, I'm truly happy in my own skin? If so, well done you! But I'd say for most of us, it's a bit of a struggle to feel comfortable accepting who we are. We have high expectation of what we should be and put unnecessary pressure on ourselves to be 'it' and when 'it' doesn't materialize, we start to hate ourselves for our perceived lack of success. We get disappointed and let the negative chatter in our heads take over to the point of disliking who we are.

They say beauty is only skin deep, but it's so much more than that. It's about being true to yourself and happy in your own skin. Somehow, today beauty carries a superficial label that is propped up by approval from others. We tend to believe if someone is popular, has the looks or charisma, they are happy, which can be so far from the truth. The truth is that there are many popular and charismatic people who are insecure, depressed or unhappy in their skin.

True beauty is about loving who you are, accepting the flaws and understanding that no matter what happens, it's OK to have doubts and make mistakes as long as we don't make them our default setting. We spend too much time worrying about body image and how we look rather than accepting who we are and being OK with it. Body image and looks has become the judgement criteria for whether or not you are of value. This is bullshit!!

I've been in the fitness industry for over twenty years and sadly, aesthetics and body image have been at the forefront of the industry for most of that time. Over the last few years, it has got a little better due to more awareness of mental health but there is still a huge emphasis on body image used as promotional material. Look at any fitness website, magazine or product and you'll see beautiful bodies promoting the story of success equalling confidence. I wish that was true, but I've seen many a person achieve great results yet still be unhappy. Weight loss, a slim waist or big muscles might make you *look* good, but it doesn't guarantee confidence nor happiness. Using body image and comparison to others to promote health is counterproductive and often destructive. The industry needs to be more accountable in its approach to body image and shift the emphasis from bodies and biceps equalling happiness to a more wholistic approach of being comfortable in your own skin no matter how you look.

How do we do that?

Feeling good in your own skin doesn't happen instantly. It's a work in progress and in that process, there are many things to consider. Most of them have nothing to do with looks, weight loss or a slim waist. Like all journeys of change, we need to start with our head. We need to understand how we think, act and talk about ourselves then learn to manage that. We can be doing all the right things needed to get into shape but if you think and talk negatively about yourself, being happy is always going to be a struggle. Your thinking and behaviour is vital to your outcome and, if not managed properly, may become the very thing that holds you back. Only when we change our thinking, do we start to change our behaviour.

Your behaviour is determined by your thinking so learn to shut out the external noise and distractions and focus on your strengths instead of your weaknesses. This will help build confidence. By building confidence and using positive self-talk, your chance of being comfortable in your own skin increases. Who knows where that will lead?

Being comfortable in your skin and learning to like your own company is powerful. We need to stop looking for approval and validation to feel we are good enough. Validation and approval are some of the strongest motivating forces that influence our behaviour. They're often the base for the decisions we make and, depending on how we control them, determine the way we act.

Be it on a small or large scale, there's no denying that we all seek some form of approval or recognition, whether it's posting to receive a like on social media, doing something outrageous to be noticed or saying something clever to make an impact. I'm sure at some stage we've all acted in a way hoping to get a reaction and, most probably, one of approval or recognition.

Why do we do it?

Recognition and acceptance make us feel wanted and good about ourselves, which boosts our perceived self-worth, especially if or when it supports our beliefs or actions. Frequently we do this, whether it be at home, at work, with friends or people we don't even know, and sometimes we're not fully aware we're even doing it.

Is it wrong to seek approval or validation?

That depends on why you seek it. There are times when seeking approval or validation isn't a problem. Let's face it, you can't always be positive or certain all of the time, so the occasional pick-me-up when feeling a little flat or you need to know you're on the right track can be a good thing.

Where it's not a good thing is when your self-worth is based on it. Some people constantly seek the approval of others and will go to great lengths to get it, even to the point of going against their own values or beliefs. Your ego might get stroked in the short term but how long can you keep the façade going before you realise that it's disempowering?

Seeking approval is tiring work, especially if you're trying to please everyone. Remember, there's bound to be someone who'll disapprove. Let go of the fear of disapproval and start believing in yourself! Take some risks! Try new things! Stop worrying whether others will approve or not! The sooner you realise you don't need the tick of approval to be yourself, the easier life becomes. Open the door to the real *you* because you don't need someone else to open it for you!

It's time to ignore the marketing hype and the media noise of what is *acceptable beauty* and connect with being happy in your own skin. Approval, validation, a beautiful body, big biceps, or a slim waist might make you look or feel good, but it doesn't guarantee happiness. True happiness isn't about living up to expectations, comparing yourself to others, body image, or approval. It's about being true to yourself and learning to be comfortable in your skin. As in the words of Bruce Springsteen's song *Better Days*, '*It's a sad man my friend who's living in his own skin and can't stand the company.*'

CHAPTER 3:
Fakes, Failures and Falsehoods

Fakes

Our obsession with success, fame or wealth and what it can bring has led us down the rocky road of what's real and what's fake. Just turn on the news, Internet or any social media platform and it's full of people spruiking their story of success and how, by following their plan, it can be yours too. We buy into their self- promoting story, especially when it's backed by photos. We trust their credibility because, somehow, a picture makes it more believable! We admire their confidence, success and happiness and see them as a source of inspiration. We then follow their posts with adoration, respect, and sometimes addiction, without really questioning the validity of their story or whether it's actually true. We live in a culture where we put our trust in people because they have a profile without questioning their credibility or qualifications. We follow self-proclaimed gurus who use their status and charismatic stories and this gives us a false sense of security.

It's easy to think someone is an expert or a success especially when they appear to have celebrity status or lots of fans. We need to look beyond the hype and glamour to find the truth behind what we see because it could be a completely different story. How many celebrities, influencers, actors, musicians, health and fitness or personal development gurus have we put on a pedestal because they appeared to be genuine, likeable and trustworthy, then watched them fall from grace after they've been outed for who they really are and then wonder how we got caught in their web of deceit?

We like to think we're smart and can pick someone who is fake. Sometimes we let our guard down when we follow herd mentality because a celebrity or a so-called expert appears successful, sincere and of course so much better than us. We want to be part of their tribe or follow the mob because somehow it makes us feel better, without even considering the truth. By the way, not all of these people are fakes or frauds. In fact, some work very hard in their chosen field and are well worth following but we need to be aware of what's genuine and what's good marketing with no real credibility.

There are so many examples of famous people who we've admired and put our trust in only to later discover they have lied, cheated or are fake. Take, for example, the Lance Armstrong's comeback from cancer story and his seven Tour de France wins that fooled everyone. He was the central part of one of the biggest conspiracies in sporting history. His legendary status was created behind the story that he never doped and was clean so we held him as the true sporting icon whose incredible story had such a feel-good factor about it. Why wouldn't you believe it? We bought into his amazing story and admired the honourable work he was doing for cancer, only to be taken for a ride (see what I did there? ☺) by the lies and deceit that covered up an incredible con job and that, for some, was devastating. We wanted to believe his story because deep down it gave us a sense of hope. Who doesn't relate to the underdog who comes back from adversity and proves the critics wrong to become a success? It's was such a feel-good story that we never really questioned the credibility of it because we wanted to trust and connect with it. The saddest part of this story is not that we were conned by the story but that someone would go to such extremes for the price of fame.

We're all looking for inspiration or incentive to help us be, do, or have better and we search in the hope that we can find someone or something to model ourselves on. There are copious amounts of resources to help us to become a better version of ourselves. You find them on podcasts, workshops, books, YouTube videos, social media, face to face/online courses, mentors, coaches, you name it. Who or what you use to get there, depends on your preference. There are some awesome people doing some wonderful things in this space and then there are others who are fakes. We need to be aware of those who use their status and fancy marketing to self-promote themselves and their product just to make money.

As I said, the self-help business is a billion-dollar industry and there are copious amounts of self-help information, people and products on the market to choose from so knowing the difference between what's genuine and what's not is the first step in helping yourself. If there was a person, product or method that had the answer to the self-help conundrum then I think we'd all be onto it and the self-help industry wouldn't be the money-making machine it is today. The industry is full of fakes who prey on the gullible who are willing to pay big dollars in the hope that someone will change them through some quick, easy, instant, or effortless method to change. Here's the tip. Just because someone appears to be successful doesn't necessarily mean they're genuine. Often, they're more about financial gains than your success. We need to stop wasting our money and time on people proclaiming to have the answer and learn to trust that we're good enough to avoid getting conned. The reality is, self-help is exactly that, **'self-help'!**

Just because someone is doing well doesn't necessarily mean they are happy. There are so many stories of the person who appears to be flying and in charge of their life only to find out that they are struggling to the point of depression or are even suicidal. We look upon these people and wish we had what they've got yet seldom stop to see the real picture. How many times have you read a story about a sportsperson who, at the top of their game, didn't really enjoy the moment because they felt so pressured to perform? The very thing we admire about them or wish for, is what they struggle with most. We tend to put these people on a pedestal because, from our perspective, their life looks great yet don't realise they may be struggling with anxiety or depression or feel like a fake. We think just because they are good at their craft, have a profile and appear to be doing well, they have it all together and they're happy.

The same goes for motivational gurus. We look up to them for inspiration, hoping they'll have the answers or fix us without even checking their credentials. We buy into their story because we want some of what they have, and it looks far more exciting than our uninteresting life. I went to a business seminar and the speaker up the front of the room (who apparently had won business awards) spoke about how if we follow his steps to success, we too could have all this as pictures of his lavish lifestyle were flashing up on the screen behind him. It was a bit over the top. He lost me quite early in the piece but to some, he was an inspiration and they bought, big time, into his story. It was fascinating to watch. To me, the more he spoke, the more insincere he became. He lost my trust. I later did some research on him and he had gone bankrupt, closed his business and was in a lot of debt. He was a good salesperson and yes, he told a believable story, but he was a fake with little credibility trying to make a buck out of gullible people looking for a quick fix solution.

People try to sell success as if it's a product you buy off a shelf at the supermarket. They'll tell you how success is easy to achieve if you use their method or techniques. You see it all the time using lines like, *'Earn $500 a day with little or no experience',* or *'I was a millionaire by the age of 27 and you can be too'* to entice you into their sales web of scams and upselling. I'm not against people trying to make a buck but if you're going to spend your hard-earned cash, I'd suggest you do some research and find someone who is credible and genuine so you spend your money wisely.

Another area where it's a good Idea to do your research before handing over your hard-earned cash is the health and fitness industry. Just type in the words *weight loss* and in 0.64 seconds, you'll have 1,650,000,000 results. This is amazing but also extremely daunting because how the hell do you sort the genuine from the fakes? The weight loss space is huge (pardon the pun). A lot of it is fake and based on guilt selling. What do I mean by that? I'm sure you've seen the ads for weight loss: *lose weight the easy way, lose 15 kilos in 8 weeks*, or *get thin today*. Many are endorsed by a doctor or celebrity and glossed up with some before and after photos that tell a story about their journey of success. It's well designed and even inspiring and for anyone who struggles with their weight or is wanting to lose some, it's a red rag to a bull. The problem is knowing whether it's genuine or fake. Sadly, for most people, they only find out after purchasing the product. The take home message is before you throw your money away, do some investigating to see whether the product is genuine or not.

Another area where there are many charlatans is the business industry. It too is well designed to entice you into their marketing web, using guilt and shame to inspire you into action. Since being in the fitness industry, I've been to many seminars on how to build a better business, brand, product blah blah blah. Some are good, some not so. I found it interesting how some used guilt as their marketing tool, using terms like: *'If you're not using this product, you'll be left behind'* or *'If you're aren't doing things this certain way, your business will never grow.'* I find it an interesting approach which, for some, may inspire them to take action due to their fear of failure but I believe none of these suggestions are a great long-term strategy for building a business. It's actually quite a negative approach based on comparison and feeling bad because of what you're apparently not doing. It isn't sustainable or healthy. The guilt approach haunted me for many of my earlier years of business. I was constantly comparing myself to other people and businesses and questioning why I wasn't as big or successful as they were. I was forever mentally beating myself up because someone else appeared to be doing so much better than me.

During this time, I spent time with a friend and mentor in the industry who was extremely generous and helpful with his time, advice and guidance. He was amazing! As my business grew and I was starting to implement similar strategies and mentor other people the same way, I couldn't help feeling like a fake. Looking back, it is kind of sad how I wasted so much time comparing myself to my mate and others in the industry, and feeling guilty about giving advice because I believed I wasn't a success yet, rather than using my experience to help others and focusing on doing my best.

Constantly comparing ourselves to others is a double-edged sword. It can be a driving force to enable you to become better or more successful or it can have a negative impact that leaves you feeling guilty about your lack of success. Sadly, for me in those early days, it had a negative impact which made me feel inadequate and an imposter. I was hoping if I could do the same and achieve success like my mate, my fears of feeling like a fake would disappear, therefore I'd be happy. Feeling like a fake is horrible. You're forever worried that you'll be exposed or found out and therefore considered a cheat or a liar. I don't think the thought or feeling of looking like a fake or an imposter ever goes away but you learn to manage it better and hopefully not let it interfere or restrict you as much.

Failures

Most times failing is viewed as something negative, something to avoid or not talk about. You don't see too many people going around saying, *'Awesome, I failed again!'* In fact, I don't know too many people who like to fail. The thing is, you're going to fail and probably many times throughout life which is OK as long as you don't make it a habit. The irony is failure sometimes can be the very thing that brings you success.

Let me explain: ....

We all make mistakes and get things wrong. It's a part of life. Yet, even though we know this, we still get disappointed. Ever had that sickly feeling in your stomach when you know you've made a mistake or failed? You just want to crawl into a hole to disappear for a while. Right? As much as it's upsetting and sucks big time, it can actually be what's needed for you to produce something better.

When I first started in the fitness industry, I was asked to take an aerobics class because the usual instructor had just cancelled and they urgently needed someone to take the class. The owner of the gym was in a panic. People were waiting and, regrettably, I was the only person left to do it. I'd been a gym instructor for two weeks, had no idea or interest in how to run an aerobics class, had no music to suit the class and, worst of all, the participants adored their regular, albeit absent, instructor. Being realistic you could say my chances of being successful weren't looking good. The owner assured me that it would be fine. How wrong he was. The class was an absolute disaster! In fact, it was so bad that a few people actually walked out halfway through it while letting me know how bad I was. To say the least, I was shattered, embarrassed to the point of shame. I remember driving home contemplating whether I could face these people again and whether a career in the fitness industry was really for me.

That experience of being a huge failure was a massive blow to my confidence. My dreams of a career in fitness had just been shattered. I had to decide whether to continue on that path or to go back to my previous career, which was comfortable and paid well. I decided to pick my pride up off the floor, do some reassessing and start again.

Failing is a bitter pill to swallow especially when it leaves you humiliated or feeling as if you're not good enough. As much as it hurts, failing can be one of life's best teachers. Failing is an important part of the personal development process and a test to see if you're willing to learn and grow from those experiences. It teaches you lessons that you just can't learn from books.

Although the experience was painful, it taught me some wonderful lessons. Just because things don't go as planned or you failed at something, doesn't mean you're a failure. Sometimes it may just mean you may need more practice, a better understanding, or some support to do it better next time. Yes, it's uncomfortable and at times confidence crushing but, as ironic as it may seem, failing may be just the ticket to creating the best possible you.

Here's why.

You learn to:

- **Be stronger**
  If everything were easy, we'd all be champions.
  Failure teaches us that things do go wrong and that's ok. The strength comes from accepting the loss and being determined enough to adapt and try again.
  Some of the best teams have had to overcome many defeats to find the way to win.
- **Work harder**
  Failing can be a great indicator to let us know that maybe you need to keep trying or be more thorough to avoid it happening again. It can be the inspiration or incentive to do better, be more creative and prevent reoccurrences.
- **Discover humility**
  Success is awesome and can also be a great ego booster. Be proud of your achievements but never let your ego get too big that you lose touch with what's

important. Failure is a great leveler. It can deflate the ego very quickly, so learn to enjoy the wins but be humble in the celebrations.

- **Finding who your real friends are**
  They say success breeds success, but it also attracts pseudo friends and fans. You'll have plenty of backslapping admirers when the going is good but your real friends appear when you need them most.

- **Being adaptable**
  Even with the best laid plans, things don't always work out. Therefore, learning how to be adaptable is vital in creating better outcomes. When you understand that failure is often part of the learning process, you learn how to reduce the pressure you put on yourself and find ways to adapt to the situation.

It would be brilliant if we never had to fail but the reality is, we're going to experience it somewhere throughout the journey we call life. We live in a world where things can and will go wrong and yes, that sometimes might mean failure. Unfortunately, failure is seen as a negative experience that suggests we're not good enough, whereas if we view failure as a great opportunity to learn, grow, ask better questions, find solutions, try something different or discover a new way, the pressure and anxiety around performance would be less. We need to learn to be OK with failure and understand you're not always going to be successful but as long as you can learn from the experience and keep trying and find ways to be better, it's surely a good thing.

Falsehoods

As we have established by now, success is different for everyone and how you go about it is purely up to you. There is no right or wrong when it comes to pursuing success. Unfortunately, plenty of people will have a different opinion to you which helps to create the confusion, falsehoods and myths that surround success and how to achieve it. People love to give their idea or version of how to be successful. You'll get all sorts of tips and advice, some good and some not so. The thing is: yes, there's a plethora of information you can take on board to get you on the path to success but it's knowing what is valid for you and what's not that will help defuse the confusion. There are so many falsehoods and myths when it comes to being successful and to cover them all would be a book **in** itself so I'll pick the one I consider most common and explain why I believe it adds to the pressure and creates anxiety when we are in the pursuit of success.

Everyone thinks that hard work is the secret to success. But is it? How often have you heard someone say work hard and success will follow? Yes, you'll never be successful if you don't do the work but just because you work hard doesn't necessarily mean success is guaranteed. I remember when I was in the trade, I disliked being on the tools and wanted to get out, so I did further studies to increase my chances of getting a position in the office. This, by the way, was a lot of hard work which I thought would help me achieve my goal of getting off the tools and into the office. I was wrong. It did the opposite. When I applied for a position in the office as a leading hand, my application was rejected because my foreman thought I was a more valuable asset on the tools due to my welding certificates and greater understanding of the structural work. The point is: you can't argue that I worked hard towards what I was hoping would bring success but my efforts produced the opposite result.

You could find many positives in my predicament but for me, it seemed a lot of hard work had gone into what I considered such a poor outcome. I became so disappointed that my effort had not led to the outcome I wanted that it became the catalyst for change, and I resigned.

You can be anything you want

I get annoyed when I hear this statement because it's not just wrong, it's irresponsible and delusional. If someone is a crap singer and wants to make the big time, most times no matter how much practice and hard work they put in, the chances of them ever making the big time, are minimal. For example, as a kid I wanted so badly to be a professional soccer player that I would spend hours upon hours honing my skills to fulfil that dream. I never got the chance to pursue my dream. The opportunity never eventuated. The thing is, you may be good, even excellent at something and it doesn't matter how hard you work or how badly you want it, a thought or strong desire doesn't guarantee success. This type of thinking is delusional. It's like believing in Santa Clause, which is based on wishing for something and believing it will happen because you deserve it. Hello disappointment!

Overnight success

*'If it was an overnight success it was
one long hard, sleepless night.'*

Dicky Barrett

It's quite interesting how people or businesses are referred to as an overnight success. It's as if they were no one and suddenly out of the blue they're a success. The truth is what most people call overnight success is actually someone realising the need or value of a product or service that has gone unnoticed for a long time even though the person making it has been grinding away tirelessly and refusing to give up and now, suddenly, the potential of their idea is recognised. They've most times dedicated years to learning and perfecting their craft, often experiencing failure, disappointment and sometimes even reinvention to get to this point. We love to think of it as an overnight success because it somehow gives us hope that maybe it could be us. There are probably thousands of people stuck in front of their electronic devices hoping to be discovered as the next big thing. The thing is, overnight success does not exist, at the very least, it is so rare you have a better chance at winning the lottery.

Just because you set a goal or have ambition, doesn't mean you deserve success

When I first started my business, I was renting space within a gym and my business was moving slowly. The gym owner suggested I talk to a guy who was running another business also within the gym. He said he's going to be successful because he was confident, ambitious and believed in his goals and maybe I could learn from him how to be successful. I followed his advice and yes, he was confident and ambitious. In fact, he spoke with such conviction, using the motivational jargon like 'Believe it and you'll achieve it' and 'Build it and they will come' etc, which sounds great but is that what made him successful? To cut a long story short, unfortunately his business folded and what was sadder was a few weeks later I found a card in his room from his partner which read, 'Dream big sweetheart, I know you'll be successful because of your passion, ambition and belief in what you want to do.' Such lovely and inspiring words from someone who cared and wanted it to see it happen but the reality is, life doesn't care if it happens or not and as much as the theory makes us feel good, it doesn't always give us what we hope for.

Sometimes there is a lot of emphasis placed on goal setting and visualisation of what you want to achieve with little emphasis on the doing. Setting goals and visualising is a great start but it's just theory and life isn't lived in the theory. It's in the doing. It's like the person who joins a gym. They feel good about the theory of getting into shape yet when it comes to the application, they never actually make the effort to go. It's as if the signing up and the thought of getting in shape is good enough to produce results. Just joining a gym doesn't get you into shape. It's actually about turning up and doing the work. We need to move away from the idea that just because you set goals and think positively you have the formula for success. Yes, having a plan and believing in it is helpful but hoping for success without any action will most times lead to disappointment.

Success makes all your problems disappear

Being financially secure, professionally successful and loved, should be a great basis for happiness but it's possible to have all these things and still be pretty miserable. How many times have you read stories about the person who appears to have it all, yet is lost? Or the celebrity who is so popular yet is suffering from depression to the point of being suicidal? We take these people at face value and think how good would it be to be like them when, if we looked deeper, we'd see a different picture where the pressure of their life is wearing them down and is the very thing that's causing them unhappiness.

I remember one of my clients who was majorly depressed and had lost a heap of weight due to life circumstances. Many of my other clients were commenting on how great she looked and wanted to know the secret to her success. Truth be known, her life circumstance had her so stressed she was hardly eating and was rapidly losing weight from all the pressure she was under. People assumed because she'd lost so much weight she was doing well and all her weight issues were gone and they wanted to know her secret. Whenever someone would ask me about her assumed success and how they can do the same, I would respond with, 'Believe me, you definitely don't want to be on the plan she's on.' Isn't it funny how people assumed her weight loss meant success and that therefore her problems were solved?

We have this belief that success is the thing that'll make all our problems disappear and once we achieve success everything will be wonderful and we'll be eternally happy. Tell that to the highly successful corporate professional whose marriage is a mess and their children don't like them, or the sports star who lives a life of stress and insecurity due to the pressure of performance and expectations. These are common examples of how success can sometimes exacerbate a problem, not solve it. We love to think that just because someone is at the top of their game, they'll have less problems where most of the time that success can come at a cost.

Success is a destination

I'm sure you would've heard the quote, 'Success is a journey not a destination.' It's a bit cliché but clichés are often true. We like the notion of success being a journey yet plan it as if it's a destination and one which is set in concrete. Success as a destination is difficult for many reasons: our personal landscape is forever changing, we are constantly experiencing states of learning or unlearning, we are gaining or losing confidence, we are happy or sad, or are strong or vulnerable. Whatever the circumstance, our life is forever being transformed. According to life career change statistics, the average person will change their career 5–7 times in their working life. This alone is proof enough to suggest that success isn't a destination. If the average person changes their career that many times, then following a set path to a destination is highly unlikely.

How many times have you heard the story of the person who went to university to become a doctor, lawyer, teacher, or to pursue a vocational path because of the influence of their peers, parents or advisors? They wanted to keep these people happy or get their approval, only to realise it's not what they, themselves want so they change direction. I've met many people who, after years of working in the corporate space, have decided to make a career change into personal training to gain more balance in their lives and I also know of others who have done the opposite because other opportunities have presented themselves. Other times we change our destination because our thinking or focus has changed, we need a new challenge, we're not happy or realise that what we're doing no longer resonates or aligns with our values. I can speak from experience. I left school and started an apprenticeship in a trade I disliked because I wanted to earn money and become independent. I then became a sports/remedial massage therapist and soon realised I couldn't see myself being in a room for the rest of my life, so moved onto personal training and started my business, eventually employing other trainers, only to downsize the business and move from the huff and puff training to specialising in working with people in the disability space. At the beginning of that journey my success destination was to complete my apprenticeship and become a qualified tradesperson so I could earn the big bucks. Not in my wildest dreams would I ever have thought I'd be doing what I'm doing today and to take it a step further: writing my second book.

As you can see, there are many reasons why people change direction in life so to set success as a destination is very restrictive and doesn't fully allow for the things we experience and learn along the way that empower us to change our trajectory for the better.

You need to be ruthless to be successful

Being ruthless to achieve success does not resonate with me at all. It's often used as an excuse for people to be callous or unethical in their pursuit to becoming successful. Yes, sometimes you need to be stern and maybe a little assertive to get to the front but to be uncaring and ruthless, I believe isn't necessary.

I've always had the philosophy of ''Treat people the way you'd like to be treated.' I'd like to think that in our society today we have become more understanding and caring in our approach to reaching our goals and attaining success. Hopefully, the days of selfishness and taking advantage of others to get ahead are on the way out and people are starting to understand that through working together and empowering others, the journey of success is far more enjoyable.

As a tradesman, I remember working for a company that treated their employees badly, to the point that team moral was extremely low and respect for the company was extremely poor. How they ever thought this was a good strategy for success, to treat their workers with such disrespect yet not understand why their employees were leaving, was mind blowing. During my time there I was fascinated by the company's lack of awareness on how they treated their employees and why they struggled to keep employees long-term. It fascinated me so much that I asked the owner (with tongue in cheek) what he believed his formula for success was. This was a very interesting conversation. His response was, 'You've got to be ruthless to make it in business otherwise you'll been seen as soft and people will take advantage of you.' He proceeded to tell me that the success of the business was due to the way he managed it. He saw himself as a great leader because he was tough and the job got done. To me this was bizarre because, to us his management skills were the problem. He was inflexible, disrespectful, he micromanaged and had little awareness of how to get the best out of people. His ruthlessness may have got the job done but it also created a toxic environment that was based on fear. This created a lack of loyalty and respect that was actually restricting the company from reaching its full potential.

I'm sure there are some cases where being ruthless has produced success but the majority of business success, especially today, is based on building a good team who feel they are trusted, respected, valued and enjoy what they are doing because it has significance to them. Take Richard Branson. He is not only highly successful, he's a great leader too. He has a great understanding and awareness of what creates success. He builds teams that share the same core values, are encouraged to take risks, feel valued and are proud to be part of something bigger than themselves. Richard Branson's approach to creating success is proof that you don't need to be ruthless to create success. He has proven that being sincere and interested in people and encouraging them to be part of why you do what you do, creates a far better outcome than the ruthless, selfish and egotistical approach. In the words of Simon Sinek, *'People don't buy what you do. They buy why you do it.'*

Success doesn't come easy and sadly there are no simple and easy steps that can guarantee it either. Yet we continue to spend millions of dollars each year in the belief that success is easy. Spending money on your personal development is a sound investment but not if you're being scammed or conned. There will always be people willing to take your money. That's why having an awareness of the fakes and fraudsters helps you sort through the bullshit to get to what's real. The thing is, you can't trust everything you see, hear or read because sometimes the self-help industry is full of the hype and noise of fakes and fraudsters selling their quick and easy version of success. You know the saying, 'If it's too good to be true', you're most probably right and it's most probably a scam. Stop looking for the quick and easy way. Do the best you can with what you have and most of all, enjoy the journey.

We are all broken to some extent. It's not about whether you make it or fake it. What happens to you and around you is your story and you just have to keep trying. Life can be a bitch and it doesn't care whether you're a fraud, failure or a success, it just carries on. This is me hoping to inspire you with a motto I use when I'm struggling, and things aren't going as well as I hoped. **Life's a Bitch and then You TRY!**

CHAPTER 4:
Compound Interest and Values

Compound interest

How good would it be if you could be debt free and know you have the formula to stay debt free? I'm guessing most of us would take that in a heartbeat. The thing is, it's doable when approached the right way. I'm a big fan of The Barefoot Investor and one of his rules for reducing debt is compound interest. Compound interest is based on starting off small and consistently making deposits into your account and then being patient enough to see it grow over time. Too often people are impatient when it comes to reducing debt and choose to take what they consider the easy way on risky ventures and often find themselves losing money or in financial stress.

The compound interest is a not only a very effective money management strategy, it can be applied in many areas of our life, especially when setting goals. It's about doing the little things consistently to help you reach your goal. It's safe and allows you to start off small and gradually build momentum. It's a bit like a snowball rolling down the hill. As it builds momentum it's collecting more and more snow to eventually become something significant. For example, whenever we want to change something in our life or create better, most people either look for an easy way and hope things will work out or try to change too much and get overwhelmed or disappointed when things don't go to plan. Whereas, by applying the compound interest approach, you allow yourself to start off small, build confidence and create the momentum to keep growing, which helps increase your chances of success.

In my first book *Frustration Point,* I used the analogy of pursuing success as a wide, flowing river with water too treacherous to swim across. You are on one side (the life you want to change) and wanting to get to the other (a better life). There are two approaches: you can take a running leap across the river and hope the hell you make it to the other side, or you can be more methodical and build a bridge brick by brick, which eventually gets you safely to the other side.

Most of us want the quick fix so we take the running leap, realise it's far too risky, get scared and stay safe on the bank, settling for a life of frustration. Whereas approaching the river using the compound interest approach, you patiently build that bridge piece by piece and most times not only arrive safely, but you get to enjoy the process along the way.

In the early days of my business when things were slow, I used to sit around hoping that business would increase. My enthusiasm and expectations were high. I believed that my business would grow quickly and be a success because I was good at what I did and was passionate about it. I was believing that I could take that leap into the business world and make it easily to the other side. In hindsight, I believed my skills and enthusiasm would be enough to make it all come to fruition, only to realise there was so much more to business than skills and enthusiasm. Once I re-adjusted my thinking, lowered my expectations and started applying the *compound interest* philosophy, things slowly began to happen. This approach allowed me to create a base to work from and as those foundations became stronger, so did my confidence. This helped reduce the anxiety surrounding my slow start. I discovered that the compound interest approach allowed me to enjoy the process of growing my business within my capabilities.

Over the years working in the health and fitness industry, I've seen way too many businesses start with great enthusiasm only to fail in a relatively short time. According to the Australian Bureau of Statistics, more than 60 per cent of small businesses stop their operation within the first three years. I believe one of the reasons this happens is because they know they're good at what they do, are passionate about it, so they decide to take the risky leap without any real plan or strategy, hoping they'll make it to the other side. I'm not suggesting don't take any risks because it has worked for some but judging by the statistics above and what I've witnessed, there are way too many people drowning in that river than getting to the other side.

Whenever I think of compound interest, the Paul Kelly song, '*From little things big things grow*' gets stuck in my head. It's a wonderful protest song about indigenous struggle for land rights and reconciliation but to me, it's also a song about having values, living by them and being patient. Vincent Lingiari (an Aboriginal stockman who became a land right activist) was patient and gradually built a momentum that became so strong it started a revolution that eventually changed legislation. Lingiari had strong values and was never going to let anyone undermine or disregard them even under threat or the lure of money. When you have strong values and know what you want, you find significance and patience to know that compound interest will get you to the other side.

Compound interest is an extremely powerful tool and if more people used it as a formula in life, I believe they would be less anxious about what they want to be, do and have. To know what you want in life is vital to your success and one of the best ways to make that happen is to be like Vincent: to have values, to live by them and to do the little things to make them grow.

Values

Ever been in a situation where a person does something and you think, 'Ethically that's wrong', and you say to yourself, *'Man, that dude has no values.'* What's that about? This thinking shows what you consider to be your standard or rules in life, your value set. When someone doesn't play to those rules, we see it as wrong.

What is a value set?

Value sets are a very personal thing. They're what we base ourselves on, the rules and principles we choose to live by, which become the essence for who we are and want to be. They provide the foundation that influences most of our decisions and when we live in alignment with those rules, it can make an amazing difference in how we feel about ourselves.

Values are the things that are most important to us. They're the characteristics that resonate with our instincts, the core of what we believe in. They're our moral conscience and when we align with them, they become our judgement base working in conjunction with our gut instinct.

Think about choosing your friends or who you would prefer to hang out with? Think of the situation where you've met someone for the first time. You get an immediate feeling about them and subconsciously start to judge if they're a good or bad person. It's hard to tell exactly what someone is like on first impression. Yes, you get an idea of them, but you don't know their story. I believe you need to spend time with someone to really get to know and understand them before you can make that decision. This is where your value set kicks in. After you've spent adequate time with a person you get to see how they think, react and behave and if it doesn't align with your values you then decide whether they're someone you want to be friends with or not. Bizarrely, most times your gut is right but it's your value set that confirms that feeling.

What are the benefits of values?

If you're like me, you probably don't like making mistakes or feeling guilty and will do whatever it takes to avoid it. One of the best ways to reduce the chance of this happening is making decisions based on your value set. Our values become our guidelines for our thinking, reactions and behaviour. Whenever we are challenged with a difficult situation or decision, we refer to these values and if things don't align with them, most times we tend to base our decision on those feelings. Our decision then becomes our choice, not one that is determined or influenced by others. Living true to our values helps eliminate the complexity that often surrounds decision making. The more attuned we are to our values, the easier decision making becomes. Being attuned to your values also provides you with other benefits such as:

- Finding purpose and people who support your aspirations.
- Increasing your joy and happiness.
- Supporting your growth and development.
- Helping in times of conflict or confusion.
- Increasing your confidence.
- Reducing clutter, complexity and stress.
- Providing motivation.

To some extent our values become part of our gut instinct. When our world aligns with our values, we become more aware of our surroundings and then our spatial and situational awareness increases, making it more likely that we make decisions quicker and are comfortable with them.

Whenever I'm challenged with a situation that requires me to make a decision, I like to refer to my value set and, based on that, decide what to do. Below is an acronym for my values:

P.H.A.R.F.S. (Passion, honesty, attunement, respect, fun, and simplicity). I'll explain each in point form:

Passion – It must be something I'm genuinely interested in, will commit to and stick with.

Honesty – All parties need to be upfront and genuine in all aspects of a relationship.

Attunement – Being able to recognise, feel and connect with my surroundings and other people's emotional state.

Respect – It must be reciprocal for it to work.

Fun – Not take myself or life too seriously. It's about enjoying the moment.

Simplicity – Being minimalistic, reducing complexity and keeping things simple.

So, when decision making, I'll often refer to these and if all or majority of my values align, it'll most likely be a yes.

Over the years I've had many offers for different business ventures and each time I've referred to my values and asked whether they align with the offer and then decide if it's worth pursuing. One particular case was a partnership with another trainer. It all sounded good and definitely had the potential to work. As we started negotiating, I started to ask myself questions based on my values and discovered, although the venture had potential, it didn't align with many of my values. For example, the venture was too complex, which took away the fun element. I also wasn't totally passionate about it and didn't feel committed to it for the long-term. Based on that alone, I had to respect the other person, be totally honest with them about how I felt and say no to the venture. The thing was, although the venture was exciting and had potential, it didn't align with my values so in the end I could walk away feeling comfortable with my decision.

Here's the rub, we may not always be right but I'd say ninety per cent of the time if we are aligned with our values and listen to our gut, we'd make better decisions and feel so much happier. It's not just about being right or being in alignment, it's also about finding what's important in your world and doing the things that make you feel good. We need to simplify things and rediscover who we really are and the best way to do that is to work out what your value set is. In doing so, most times, you will find significance and discover the real you.

Your identity

Who am I?

You may be referred to as a father, a mother, a wife, a husband, a brother, a sister, a daughter, a son, married, single, a teacher, a builder, a doctor or a nurse, whatever, but is it who you really are?

We give ourselves titles that describe our position in the world and yes, they identify us but are they our identity? Which raises the question—outside of your given title, **what is your identity?**

Who you are is unique. You have a mind, body and soul of your own. You are an individual, a product of your own thoughts, behaviours, expressions, and feelings.

Having an identity is a good thing, especially when you can accept, understand and be comfortable with it. Sadly, for some it can be the very thing that holds them back. They struggle with who they are, feel trapped by their title and live life according to what that encompasses or what others perceive or want them to be. Too often we mistake our identity with our title. We start to behave, live and act in accordance with the perception of others. We get caught up in what others want or expect us to be, so we stop being true to ourselves and lose touch with who we are.

Your identity isn't an external thing. It's the real you. Your individuality, uniqueness and values, all the voices in your head, the fear and doubt, the confidence and strength, the pleasure and pain, the sadness and happiness and all those feelings in between, the thoughts and values that only you truly identify with. Those characteristics we often hide from the world so as not to appear weak, stupid or vulnerable, which is ironic because the reality is: your identity doesn't require you to be anything but yourself.

It's easy to conform to pressure of friends, family and peers and surrender your identity just to fit in. You may start to behave differently because others appear to be smarter, happier or in control, even though you have no idea of their story. We assume just because they seem happy or appear to be in control, their identity is better than ours. Sadly, some people will perpetually struggle with owning their identity and hope for things to get better, when the truth is: things don't get better, we do.

It's time to stop comparing, competing or trying to be someone or something you're not. Do a treasure hunt on your life and find some time to work out your value set. Your identity is unique. No one else can be, will ever be, or even deserves to be, you! So, embrace your value set, respect it and most of all, own it.

How do I find my value set?

Finding or working out your value set isn't easy but, as one of my values is simplicity, I'll keep it that way. There are many different ways or methods to finding your values but the way I like to approach it is to ask myself a few questions related to my beliefs, behaviours and emotions and how they make me feel.

Here are a few questions to ask yourself to establish a base to work from:

- What do I strongly believe in and why?
- What do I like doing and why?

- What's important to me and why?
- Who's important to me and why?
- What makes me feel good and why?
- How would I like to be perceived as a person and why?

Using these questions will help you discover the things that resonate with you and asking yourself why helps establish meaning or purpose for those things. Nothing is final so make as many tweaks and changes to your list as necessary until you find the words or qualities that truly resonate with you. This gives you reason to live. Life is short and no one really knows what is on the other side of it, so to waste your precious time just drifting through life or trying to please people who probably don't really care, is not living true to yourself. To use the line from The Smith's song, *Heaven knows I'm miserable now, 'In my life, oh, why do I give valuable time, to people who don't care, if I live or die?'* We don't have to be as blunt as Mr Morrissey but finding significance is about living true to your values and spending time doing the things you like with the people you love in the places you like to be.

CHAPTER 5:
Gratitude, Acceptance and Connection

Gratitude

They say life is what you make of it. Sometimes I think we take this statement too literally and try so hard to have life organised and under control. This comes about because of our need for certainty. We love to feel safe and secure and when we don't, we become anxious and worry about our lack of control. Certainty is great but life isn't like that. Life is clunky and unpredictable and trying to make it anything else is often hard work. The thing is, as much as we need and crave certainty, we also need uncertainty. Certainty can lead to boredom and staleness where we may become too comfortable, lazy, miserable, depressed, or reluctant to change. And although uncertainty can be scary, sometimes it's in the uncertainty of life that we learn to be grateful for what we have.

Trying to control everything in life is a recipe for frustration and disappointment. It's like trying to stop the waves from rolling in by building a sand wall. Eventually it'll get worn down. We fear uncertainty therefore want to control it. We set plans and have strategies in place, hoping they'll keep things in check, only to be thrown a curve ball that we didn't see coming. Having plans and being organised is fantastic if life plays along with them but life can change in an instant and that's something we have absolutely no control over. The best we can do is design a plan based on controlling what is within our control and then adjusting and adapting to circumstances accordingly as they unfold.

The more we can allow life to play its role without trying to control it, the less stress and anxiety we'll encounter. Life happens whether you like it or not, yet we cause ourselves so much grief and unhappiness trying to control it. The amount of time we waste either living in the past or worrying about the future is pointless because we can't change nor control either. I love the quote, *'No amount of guilt can change the past and no amount of worrying can change the future.'* So, no matter what has happened or is going to happen, we have no control over it, so accept it and focus on what we can control.

Throughout life we'll encounter all sorts of unpredictable moments and uncertainty and yes, they'll most likely change the way we think and feel and, depending on how you react to them, will determine how much they affect you. In the unpredictability and uncertainty of life is often where the best lessons are taught and it's through these experiences we grow and adapt.

Travel is a perfect example because you may have plans and schedules but you never know what lies ahead and without warning things can go wrong. Over the years I've done quite a bit of travel and I love it but in saying that, it can have its moments of unpredictability and uncertainty. Like the time I went for a run in Hong Kong. I caught the ferry to Hong Kong Island and somehow lost my money so had nothing to buy a return ticket back to the mainland. At the time it was a real inconvenience and something I hadn't anticipated so I had to move out of my comfort zone and try to communicate with some locals to see if I could get some money for the return fare. Although I wasn't in danger, I had to literally ask people for money and yes it was uncomfortable. It taught me that you don't have to be fluent in a language to be able to communicate and that people are willing to help someone in genuine need because it makes them feel good. Since that day I will always pay that kind gesture forward because I was so grateful for the lady who was not only lovely and generous, she had a good sense of humour, which made the awkward moment fun.

Now I could have panicked and cracked the shits on life but it wouldn't have changed the situation. The incident wasn't anything major but the point is: life can be uncertain and sometimes it deals you a crap hand but it's not so much about the cards your dealt, it's how you play them. When life has dealt you a bad hand, it's not always easy to see them as playable but somehow, we need to find the resilience to keep playing.

What do I mean by that? You know the story where someone experiences a traumatic moment in life and feels that life just isn't fair. The truth is: life isn't fair and bad things happen to good people and you can either sit in the sadness of the event or decide to change things and make them better. Finding the resilience to keep playing the game of life is about understanding how quickly life can change and being able to accept and adapt to those changes as best you can.

That's where gratitude plays a huge role in determining how these experiences shape us. Most times we go through life just 'doing the do' until our world is rocked. Only then we decide to make some changes. This is where we start to become more aware, appreciative and grateful for what we have. The thing is: it shouldn't take a crisis for us to be grateful.

I love the movie *A Good Year*. It's about a high-flying bond trader who receives a letter that his uncle who taught him the values of gratitude and appreciation as a little boy, has passed away. The story has him leave his work for a few days and go to the south of France to attend to his deceased uncle's financial affairs. Over the years, he has become so selfish and ungrateful in his role that he's forgotten about all those values his uncle taught him. He now fears leaving his job for a few days because his ego tells him that he's far too important to be away from work. To cut a long story short, his visit makes him slow down to the point where he begins to realise how selfish and ungrateful he has become, thus he's forgotten about enjoying the simple pleasures in life. Through his epiphany, he becomes aware of his surroundings, the sights, the sounds, the smells and all the little things his present existence has made him forget. Whether the story is real or not, it's a pity that people have to go through some kind of grief to realise what they've always had. We can get so caught up in doing 'the do' that we forget about the simple things that make our world an amazing place.

The quote, *'It's only in the darkness you see the stars'* comes to mind whenever I see this occur. The thing is: the stars are always shining, it's only when you take the time to look up and notice the night sky that you begin to understand gratitude. It's a pretty wonderful thing this place we inhabit and when we understand and appreciate this amazing gift, gratitude presents itself.

Being thankful

Gratitude to me is about appreciating the simple things in life and learning to be thankful for what we have. I find it a little ironic that we really don't need much to be happy, yet people spend heaps of money buying stuff that they think will make them happy. I've seen many people with the big house, full of the latest gadgets and lovely furniture, driving around in their big cars believing it will make their world a better place. They're forever collecting stuff in the hope it brings them happiness, fills the void or worse still, to impress others.

Here's the thing: happiness isn't in the things you possess. Yes, there will be things that bring you joy and make you feel good for a while but when that feeling fades, most times you start searching again for that emotional high. Whereas if we stopped looking for bigger or better all the time and were grateful for what we have already, we'd realise most times what we have is good enough. We live in a comparison culture where we compare what we have to what someone else has and you know the result of that—the grass is somehow always greener over there. When we fall victim to the comparison culture, we begin to focus on what we haven't got therefore forget to appreciate what we already have.

Most of my work these days is in the rehabilitation/disability space and I get to see firsthand how quickly life can change. I deal with a wide variety of clients with multiple sclerosis, brain injuries, or who have had a stroke or have Alzheimer's who were once fully cognitive and able bodied and are now in a wheelchair, unable to use one side of their body or they have lost their memory. Now that for me is the daily reality check to be thankful for what I have, yet I constantly hear abled-bodied people who whinge and bang on about how hard life is or how inconvenient an injury or situation is. I know everything is relative to where we are at any particular time in life but don't expect too much sympathy from me when you're complaining about a short-term problem when I see people every day who have conditions that'll be with them for the rest of their life. Be thankful for your health and get on with life.

I'm not saying I never whinge but I'm well aware that I'm grateful to be able bodied and healthy. Sometimes we can get so caught up in our own world and focus on the negative that we forget how good we actually have it. The thought of losing my ability to move around freely, have all or some of my limbs unable to function, or my mind failing is enough to make me thankful for what I have. I can truthfully say

I'm privileged to have the opportunity to work with some of the most resilient and grateful people who have taught me to be thankful for what I have. I could be or you could be like them. Our lives could change in an instant.

Here's the rub: being thankful isn't about comparing yourself to others who are less fortunate and can still be happy, it's about having an awareness that most times who you are and what you have is good enough, and learning to be OK with that.

Slow down

My dad would use this is an expression any time we got ahead of ourselves or out of hand. He would, in his broad Belfast accent say, 'SLOW DOWN!', taking a small pause between the two words. We knew instantly we needed to pull our heads in and regain perspective. For us as kids, this was an obvious warning that we were getting close to receiving a scolding or being disciplined. Today, whenever I hear that phrase, it still reminds me of that stern warning but now it has a totally different meaning. We now live in a fast-paced and ever-changing world and it's easy to get caught up in its flow. It's good to slow down and do a self-audit to gain perspective.

You need to move with the times and keep up with the trends but not if you become so busy that you don't have time to slow down. Technology has become a huge factor in how busy we've become. Today we are constantly switched on and connected to our devices, which makes us contactable 24/7. There's nothing wrong with being connected and busy but you also need to be able to disconnect and slow down. If we're always busy, the body doesn't get time to recuperate. It's like continuously driving your car and hoping it won't break down. Something's got to give.

Being constantly switched on may sound productive but it can only be sustained for so long before the body starts to fight back. That's when we need to slow down and listen to the message our body is telling us. Our body is an amazing piece of equipment that is constantly sending us messages and you'll only hear those messages when you take the time to slow down and listen. Being busy is often seen as being productive and is worn as a badge of honour, which is a bit of a wank. There seems to be this image that surrounds busyness and success. Yes, you have to put in the work, but you also need to be smart about how you go about it. Being constantly busy increases the likelihood of fatigue and burnout and it's at that point you become non-productive.

Slowing down allows you to recharge and refocus on what's important. Too often in our busyness we get distracted by the noise and forget to take time to appreciate the little things in life. I'm a runner and for years whenever I went for a run it was all about time and distance, so you could say my runs were purely focused on the outcome. Through my travels I've been blessed to run in some awesome locations yet never really got to enjoy the environment because I was so busy with the detail. I began to realise I've run in so many great locations yet seldom stopped or slowed down to take in the view. This realisation made me change my approach to running and now I run to be more in the moment and enjoy my surroundings. Being too focused on the outcome, I missed out on some wonderful opportunities to take in the local sights and experience the special moments as they were unfolding.

Getting distracted in the busyness of life can also affect our relationships. Have you ever caught up with someone for meal or a coffee and the whole time they're constantly distracted by their phone? It's annoying and personally I think, quite rude. I get there are times when it's necessary to check your phone but letting it become more important than the person you're with, kind of defeats the purpose of the catch up. On that, you can't expect people to be 100 per cent present all of the time either but being present as much as possible is a sign of respect and you understand the power of slowing down.

At times I think dad was wiser than I gave him credit for. If I had actually slowed down and paid more attention to him, instead of thinking I knew it all, I probably could've learnt more valuable lessons earlier in life. One of those lessons would have been to put my time and energy into the people who matter most. It's ironic how much time we can waste on people or things that add minimal value. I think of the time I spent seeking approval from people that either didn't care or quickly moved on, disregarding those that care and have become lifelong friends. Life is a great teacher and it's always sending us signs and signals but it's not until we slow down and start listening that the teacher arrives.

When we stop and listen to what is going on around us, we begin to appreciate the people in our lives and the things we have. The genuine friendships I have built with my brothers is an example of this (although at times they can do my head in). The fun times and special moments we've had are priceless. When you reflect on how important these people and events are and how they make you feel, you get to fully understand the significance of gratitude.

It's at this point of realisation we become thankful, we slow down and stop taking things for granted. And the sooner we can do that the quicker we can start to find the significance in our life. We literally need to take time out to smell the roses, do more fun things and spend more time with the people we love because we only get one chance at this life and when it's gone, it's gone! I had a friend who suddenly passed away at a young age. We were forever going to catch up. Whenever we'd chat over the phone, we'd end by saying, 'Mate, we must catch up' yet never did. We always thought we'd have plenty of time so it would eventually happen. Life changed that in an instant. Now we'll never have that catch up ever again. The opportunity for two mates to sit down to talk, have a laugh and some fun won't ever be. I can be regretful that we didn't make a better effort but that's not going to change anything. All I can do is be grateful for our friendship and use that sad experience as a lesson not to make the same mistake again.

You can get annoyed at life and at times ask the question of why does life have to be such a harsh teacher but the thing is: life goes on whether you like it or not. If we are constantly in the state of noise and busyness then the chance of not hearing or seeing the signs increases. There were many times that the signals were flashing to tell us both to catch up but we took it for granted that we'll be around for a lot longer but now it's too late. The saddest thing about the situation was, we were both in a sense being busy now so we could make more time for later on. In hindsight, I can now see how flawed our plan was.

The above scenario was a wakeup call for me to be more aware of what's important and making time to enjoy them now, not in the future. When we are always on the go, doing what we believe is important right now, it's easy to disregard or take the little things that make up the big picture, for granted. Think of it like a jigsaw puzzle. It's all the little pieces that make the big picture. The thing is, we can get so engrossed in wanting to see the full picture that we forget that it'll never be complete without all those little pieces.

Acceptance

Not everything in life is going to go to plan and sometimes just when you thought you had it all under control, it all goes pear-shaped. We love certainty and predictability, but life doesn't work that way. It's not as if life isn't fair, it's just what it is. We have a choice: we can either accept it and go with the flow or resist and fight against it. You can try to resist it but most times all that creates is anxiety whereas when you learn to accept it and go with the flow, you find things aren't as bad as they seem.

Acceptance is having the ability to acknowledge the negative people, experiences, thoughts and feelings in your world without the shame, anxiety and judgement of why it's happening to you. It's not endorsing what's happening, it's recognising it for what it is and understanding that although you may not like it, have any control over it or even be able to change it, you're able to acknowledge it and be OK with that. Trying to always be in control is tiring and at times pointless. Sometimes it's better to accept the situation for what it is, rather than trying to control or get upset by it.

Anyone who has travelled knows what it's like to experience a cancellation or a travel delay. I remember a time when my wife and I were stuck in a very hot Naples railway station due to heat problems. My initial reaction was annoyance but, once we took the time to digest it, we realised there was nothing we could do to change the situation and no amount of stress or anger was going to get that train to depart any earlier. We had two choices: complain about how disruptive and annoying the situation was to our travel plans or accept that we're going to be here for a few hours so we may as well find something to occupy our time. To cut a long story short, we decided on the second option. Firstly, I found an airconditioned travel office to get out of the heat, which become our base for the next few hours, and then I got a drink and something to eat. The best thing about this experience was that we enjoyed just being in the moment. It's very interesting what you observe when you slow down enough to absorb your environment.

After a little bit of searching I eventually found a decent café. Not being in any hurry, I sat and did one of my favourite things—watched people. During this people watching episode, I was fascinated by the barista and how he conducted himself. He was amazing! Although being snowed under with orders, he did not once look flustered or stressed. In fact, he was quite chatty and very pleasant and the best bit was how skilled and in control he was. When my order was ready, I complemented him about what I'd just observed and said, 'You obviously enjoy your work.' His reply was gold. He said, 'This is a performance and I want to put on the best show I can every time.' He did and I enjoyed every minute of that show!

What's the point of that story? I had a choice on how I reacted to the event. I could have become annoyed about the delay, which would have probably put me in a worse mood, made the experience an unpleasant one and, worst of all, not changed the outcome. By deciding to go with the flow I got front row seats in this young man's show and experienced something so simple yet so enjoyable. The thing is: when we're always trying to be in control, we get so caught up in our own importance, lose the skill of acceptance and start looking for blame, rather than accepting what has just happened and improvising and adapting. As in this case, by accepting the situation for what it was and going with the flow, I was able to encounter an event I thoroughly enjoyed and in doing so, the delay to our travel plans was not only enjoyable, it was also a great learning experience!

Like the story above, my initial reaction was about control and certainty. I didn't like the fact that what was planned and was meant to run to schedule didn't pan out that way. We want life to be predictable and need to be in control, which is a massive ask because life is often quite messy but it's in that messiness, we receive the lessons to help us grow and become who we are. The messiness and mistakes we make are part of life. Learning to be OK with our regrets and mistakes is tough but it helps us to keep moving forward.

We've all made mistakes. Living in regret or shame doesn't change what's happened. I know it's all relative to the individual but, to live in regret or shame for something you, most times, cannot change, is torturing yourself. There are always things that we ruminate over and wish we could change. Let go or move on from them. Mind you, I'm sure when you're in the middle of it, the last thing you need is someone telling you to get over it or move on!

Saying that, living in the regret or shame isn't healthy either. What's happened has happened and can't be undone. By learning to accept it, isn't so much letting go or moving on, it's about trying to keep moving forward. In theory, letting go or moving on is great if you can but the reality for many is that it's not that simple. If you've ever had someone you love pass away, you'll know how badly it hurts and you wish the pain would go away. From experience, it's such a shitty feeling and I can say this feeling never really goes away. At times it'll hit you when you least expect it, which makes it very hard to let go or move on. To me moving on is like trying to shut out what is real and that's bloody hard. We need to face the truth and accept what's happened before we can even try to understand how to manage it or move on.

Living with regret or shame can be the similar. It's hard to move on from the hurt but we need to learn to manage it and find a way so we can keep moving forward. When you come to terms with what has happened and learn to be OK with it, it's not so much about moving on or even letting go, it's about moving forward and managing the situation as best you can. It comes back to wanting to have control and sometimes our emotions just won't allow that. There's a saying, 'No amount of guilt can solve the past and no amount of shame can change the future.' Accepting what is and being OK with that, is the best way of moving forward. When we learn to accept the past and keep moving forward, we tend to focus on the things we can control.

There are many things in life that are out of our control yet somehow even when we know this, we still try to control them. Trying to control what's uncontrollable is a futile exercise. We'd be better off saving our time and energy and just accepting them for what they are. This would reduce the stress and anxiety we create around it. Three areas I feel we waste a lot of energy on are: the past (as explained above), worrying about what people think, and the future.

Worrying what others think

We spend too much time worrying about what others think. We live in a world that's becoming extremely opinionated and quite divisive because of it. As democratic as we like to think we are, if someone doesn't agree with you, there's a fair chance they'll be offended or even dislike you. As much as we would love to go through life without upsetting anybody, it's impossible and if you think you can, you're a little delusional. There's a quote by John Lydgate, made famous by Abraham Lincoln, *'You can please some of the people all of the time. You can please all of the people some of the time, but you can't please all of the people all of the time.'* We spend unnecessary energy on trying to please or keep people happy because we're worried about what they might think or how we might be perceived. Believe me, we have no control over someone else's thoughts and trying to control that is a pointless, so instead of wasting energy on trying to change or please them, accept it and use your energy for better things.

Worrying about what others think is not just energy zapping, it's disempowering. Most humans desire approval or to be liked and we dread disapproval, therefore, we try our hardest to please. Wanting approval or to be liked is OK but not if it consumes your time and energy or disempowers you. There will always be people who will dislike you no matter what and who you have no control over but what you can control is how much emotional energy you spend on worrying about it. Think of a time when you said something you truly believed in and thought you were just being assertive and staying true to your values, only to later worry whether you've upset or offended someone? It's going to happen and as much as we want to be liked, there will be times where you're going to offend or upset someone, accept it and try not to waste time and energy on it.

The third area people try to control is the future. They worry about shit that hasn't even happened and most of the time probably won't. It's interesting how we plan for the future as if it's in our control. Don't get me wrong, I make plans and like having structure but I know I'm never really in control of it. Life can change in an instant and I'm OK with that. As I'm writing this, the world is going through a pandemic. The COVID-19 virus is spreading and countries are in lockdown and people are dying. Who would have predicted that at the beginning of the year? This is a perfect example of how unpredictable life can be and how quickly it can change, so to think you can have control over that, is setting yourself up for major disappointment.

Have you ever been asked the question, '*Where do you think you'll be in 5 years?*' My immediate response to this question is, 'How the hell can I honestly know?" Myself, I think it's a bit of a redundant question especially when things are constantly changing but it's a great example of why you shouldn't waste too much time and energy worrying about the future. At the beginning of this year, most of us would have been planning our yearly resolutions, goals or to-do list. We would have become excited about what lay ahead and how we're going to implement the plans and now they have been thrown into disarray. The thing is, we make our plans in the hope it gives us some kind of direction, motivation and structure. The irony is, we're planning on certainty in a world that is anything but certain.

As I've mentioned, I work in the rehabilitation/disability space and this is a perfect example of life's unpredictability. The people I work with once had what they'd call a normal life and through no fault of their own, their life changed dramatically and, for some, in an instant. I work with people with multiple sclerosis which, sometimes admittedly can be a slow, gradual change but whether the change is quick or slow, their future has changed. I also have people who, in an instant due to an accident or a medical condition, had their life turned upside down. My point: We need to understand that it's great to make plans and think about the future but to worry and try to control it, is like trying to drive a car without a steering wheel.

Being in control is wonderful. Life just seems to flow so much more smoothly when we're in control but, as we know, life's unpredictability disrupts that. Let's face it, we all would like to be in control and live as stress-free as possible. We make plans, hoping to gain control but sometimes as soon as we try to gain that control, those plans become our stressors because we realise that we actually don't have much control. Think about it, we want control so badly that we hang onto those goals, plans, to-do lists, so tightly that we may eventually become controlled by them which, bizarrely, creates stress, the very thing we try to avoid. I know, ironic hey?

We do this due to fear. Fear of the unknown, change, failure, or making mistakes and because it becomes our focus, it controls us. I remember my first overseas experience. I left my secure job and decided to hitch hike across Canada. I was a small town boy with (as I soon discovered) no real street smarts. I began this journey with lots of fears, doubts and uncertainty about what the future held and that was bloody scary. I had a plan of what I wanted or hoped to do but had no idea how I was going to manage it. As soon as I got on that plane, the security of my home, friends and familiarity weren't there anymore, all my insecurities and fears come rushing through. The fear of uncertainty and what the future held become my focus and the excitement of my plans soon became my fears. I wanted control and, to a great extent, security about what lay ahead. I was stressing about things that hadn't even happened and, fortunately, didn't. When I look back, I can't help thinking about how naïve I was to expect everything go to plan and for me be in control of the future.

Once I realised I had very little control of what lay ahead, I had to learn to be OK with that. I had to adapt and be more open-minded, to accept that I can't control the future and to learn to go with the flow and try to stay calm when things didn't go to plan. Although, during that period I had to battle a lot of my demons, in hindsight, that trip became one of the best things I ever did. The friendships, lessons, growth and the amazing experiences I encountered become the best self-awareness workshop I've ever done.

We need to accept that some things are out of our control and the more we try to control them, the more stress we'll encounter. Whereas if we let go of trying to control everything and go with the flow more, we'll, most times, experience less anxiety around those fears. Acceptance is the ability to tolerate negative thoughts and feeling, allowing yourself to feel and experience things without judgement, shame or anxiety. It's not endorsing what you're accepting but recognising it for what it is and understanding that, although you may not like it or be able to change it, you're able to be OK with it. Acceptance is being real about what's happening to, around and because of you, and being able to adapt and manage the situation as best you can. It's about having the resilience to experience the frustration of something being out of your control, yet having the awareness to accept it without too much stress or anxiety.

Connection

We all want connection and to feel we belong. It's a human need. Whether it's family, friends, groups or places, most of us need to be part of something; something that makes us feel good, accepted and valued. We are tribal creatures us humans and are hard-wired for connection. We crave to be accepted, noticed and supported because it gives us the belief that we belong to something that is bigger and more important than ourselves.

In Abraham Maslow's hierarchy of needs, belonging is one of the major needs that motivates human behaviour. This hierarchy is usually portrayed as a pyramid, with more basic needs at the base and more complex needs near the peak. The need for love and belonging sits in the middle of the pyramid as part of the social needs. While Maslow suggested that these needs were less important than the physiological and safety needs, he believed that the need for belonging helped people to experience companionship and acceptance through the relationships they build.

Healthy relationships are fundamental to our psyche. They give us purpose and meaning. They give us a place where we can be understood, share experiences, find comfort, build trust with those we connect with. We like to associate with people who are similar to us, who have similar likes, principles, ethics and understanding. We also build relationships with those who have been through or had a similar experience to us because, on some level, we feel the connection and therefore we understand each other. Then there are some relationships we form through associations like work, leisure or sport and then there are some that just evolve. No matter what the reason or circumstance we build those relationships because we feel a connection to the person or group and that gives us a sense of belonging.

As I mentioned earlier, as I'm writing this book we are going through a worldwide pandemic and have been told to self-isolate, stay in our homes and if out and about we need to practise social distancing. This, for most of us, is hard to come to terms with. As a result, people are starting to realise the importance of physical connection and the role it plays in our psyche. Although the social network platforms and video chats have increased, these formats can only fill so much of the void. The human need for physical connection is being tested and, bizarrely, the outcome is people are beginning to see how important physical connection is and how much we were taking it for granted. If anything positive comes of this crisis, I'm hoping it's that people will start to put greater emphasis on physical connections where they'll spend more time communicating face-to-face and being present, rather than having their head stuck in their devices, or worse still, being too busy to find time to catch up.

The lockdown phase has exposed some very interesting behavioural habits of society. People are now commenting on social media about how we need to show compassion, be more empathetic and support one another, share our love and start caring for others through these uncertain times. It's funny how it's not until a crisis that people start to become more grateful for what they had. This crisis has highlighted how we've become quite self-absorbed, to the point of disregarding the simple things in life and when they're taken from us, ironically, we crave them.

Why connect?

We connect for many reasons but mostly it's about how those connections make us feel. Connecting with other people is good for our physical and mental health because it provides us with a sense of security and significance. We all need security of some sort in our lives, to feel safe and to be confident that we have people who will look out for us and have our backs. You know the feeling when you have someone who makes you feel good, that person who contacts you to see if you're OK and you'd do the same for them. These are the type of people who make your world a better place, the type you just love being with because they boost your confidence and make you feel better about yourself.

There are many different reasons why we crave connection and, depending on what that connection is, determines its significance. Below is a list of the type of connections I have and a few reasons why they are significant to me.

Family

Well, you could say that you don't have much of a choice on this on because you were born into this family but actually you do. It's your choice whether you connect with family members or not. Some families just don't get on and there's very little connection between them. We all have a choice whether we want to associate with our family or not. I grew up in a family of eight boys and yes, we had our fair share of fights and arguments growing up, and occasionally still do, but I can honestly say I'm very fortunate. I'm fortunate because, even before I start to look outside of my family for connection, I have seven brothers who I totally love, trust and would do anything to support and help them whenever needed and can confidently say, I know it's reciprocal.

Growing up in a large family had its drawbacks, especially that we didn't have a lot and often struggled our way through life. To have material things just wasn't on the agenda so we had to find alternatives and in doing so, we became creative, resilient and very protective of each other. We would spend hours playing games like soccer, cricket, football, or some other outdoor activity and during that time, would chat, laugh, argue and share our experiences. This was the glue to a bond that just grew stronger and stronger to the point where it just became who we were. The trust, support and friendship we developed throughout those years is something only we know and now no matter what happens, good or bad, it will never be torn apart. I always think of The Hollies song, *He ain't heavy he's my brother* because no matter what challenges life throws at us, we do our best to carry each other through it. I could write a book just on growing up with my brothers. It had it all, the good, the bad, laughter, sadness, enjoyment, and adversity but whatever the experience, most of it was shared together and we helped each other cope, which created such deep connections.

My brothers are my best mates and, to me, this is the highest level of friendship I could ever want. I believe we were lucky to have such wonderful parents who installed such strong values and ethics into us that we all looked after and respected each other (I wish I had realised that a lot earlier in life). Just for the record, everything was perfect, in fact, at times it was far from it. Over the years we've had our fair share of disagreements and fallouts and, at times, we've given each other the absolute shits but as much as we've gone through those periods, we've never turned our back on each other. To me, and I'm pretty confident my brothers would be the same, whenever I've had a falling out with one of them, I can't help but feel ill in the stomach and as much as my pride tells me not to worry, I cannot make it go away until we have settled our indifferences and are OK again. Now that is a powerful connection!

Friends

I remember reading an article talking about friendships and it spoke of how the average Facebook user has 338 friends and Robin Dunbar, an anthropologist and evolutionary psychologist, doubted if these are indeed 'friends'. For him, an average person can have at most 150 friends with whom they can maintain a stable relationship. He adds, however, that in reality, we're only able to maintain a mere five real friendships at a time. I found this fascinating because we put a lot of emphasis on friendships and to think we can have so many friends yet effectively can only maintain very few of them.

Some people may like to disagree with that statement but if you're absolutely honest with yourself when you dig deeply into the well of your friends, how many of them would be really close and do almost anything to help you out? The reality would be, probably, not too many. Using my brothers as a basis for what friends do, I would say Robin Dunbar is right. I probably have (apart from my brothers) about four or five friends who I could absolutely count on. Now this is neither good nor bad, it's just what it is. For me, those people are genuine and trustworthy friends.

So why is it then, if we can only maintain a stable relationship with a handful of people, are friends so important? Significance! Friends are the people who add value and meaning to our lives. They support, encourage and give us the belief and confidence to become a better person. Close friends are real, honest and accept us for who we are. They'll challenge, question, and at times, annoy the crap out of us but in the middle of all that, they help us grow and gain a better understanding of ourselves.

Friends are important for so many reasons and depending on what type of person you are, those reasons will vary but to me, friends:

- Help reduce my stress levels.
- Build my confidence.
- Provide a comforting shoulder.
- Share a listening ear when needed.
- Keep me grounded with their honesty.
- Fill my world with fun and laughter.

The reason why I choose friends with these attributes is that they're good for my health, both mentally and physically. I connect with these people because they have good energy, are fun to be around and, although we don't always have to agree, we have an understanding that makes our connection meaningful.

Work associates

We spend a huge part of our day at work and if it's a place of stress and anxiety, it makes for an extremely long and tiresome day. I believe if you are going to spend so much time in the same environment you need to try and make that environment a place of good energy. Work for some is all about having your head down and getting the job done, which is fine but I'm sure that most times you could still get the work done and have some fun, which would make the job so much more gratifying. I'm not suggesting everything has to be fun and everyone has to be best friends but when I connect well with my work colleagues, my productivity, creativity and job satisfaction increases and that's good for my self-esteem. It is also why connection with work associates is so valuable.

Mentor friends

Mentors are wise beings. They just know stuff and have a wonderful understanding of the world and how to simplify it. To some they are a bit intimidating but for me, connecting with a mentor helps me understand that we're all a part of something greater than ourselves. I have a few mentors who I connect with whenever I need some guidance or support and, over the years, some of these mentors have become good friends. Connecting with my mentor friends brings the calmness and energy I need to help me regain perspective and get back on track. We can get so caught up in our own importance and busyness that we lose perspective of what's significant. Whenever I feel my frustration or ego is creating chaos, I try to speak with one of my mentor friends.

When we catch up to share our thoughts and experiences, it's about parking my ego and becoming the student who listens to understand the lesson that's being taught.

I'm lucky to have wonderful people like these as my friends. Our relationships are based on truth, acceptance and gratitude. I believe we all need mentors in our lives who can guide and teach us the value of being OK with making mistakes and messing up and to appreciate that asking for help isn't a sign of weakness or that you're dumb.

Mentor friends help slow me down and keep me grounded and grateful for the simple things in life that, when my ego takes the driver's seat, I take for granted. I also enjoy their perspectives on life because I can be sometimes be quite biased in my thinking which, at times, limits my scope for taking risks and trying new things. In my experience, I believe having a mentor friend is one of the most valuable personal growth connections you can have. To have someone who understands and cares enough about you that they'll travel on your journey yet not control the destination, teach you yet not judge your results, see your faults yet focus on your strengths and be empathetic to your emotions yet honest enough to tell you the truth, is important. It's connections like these that build resilience, confidence and the belief that who we are is of significance and to realise this, it's gold!

As you can see, there are many different types of friendships and these are the ones that resonate with me. The energy that exists between the people you trust and value is powerful and having relationships and connections that are built on that energy helps lower our anxiety, depression and loneliness, while increasing our confidence, happiness and sense of belonging. As well as fulfilling the need to belong, friendships are important to our wellbeing and play a significant role in helping us to stay connected through the good and the bad. If you've ever been through a rough patch in life, how good is it to have good friends come to help and support you through those times? That's when you really get to experience the significance of true friends.

Understanding the significance of friendships gives you a greater appreciation of why connection is important. It's OK to spend time on your own or be the lone ranger but I'm sure when adversity hits, you'll be grateful for the support and thankful you have connections.

Another need we humans crave is touch. We're tactile creatures and physical contact whether it be a pat on the back, a reassuring hand on the shoulder, or a comforting hug, is like a medicinal energy that helps boost our immune system. Lack of touch, often referred to as skin or touch hunger, plays a huge role in our wellbeing to the point of warding off mood, anxiety and immune disorders. Human touch is vital to our existence.

A study undertaken by Dr Ruth Feldman (Simms-Mann Professor of Developmental Social Neuroscience) was conducted where 73 premature babies were given maternal skin-to-skin contact and were compared to 73 babies who received incubator care. After repeated testing, from age six months to ten years, those in the skin-to-skin group were found to have greater cognitive skills. At ten years of age, these children also had better sleep patterns, physical responses to stress, more advanced autonomic nervous systems, and better cognitive control.

Another review of research, conducted by Tiffany Field, a leader in the study of touch, found that preterm newborns who received just three 15-minute sessions of touch therapy each day for 5-10 days gained 47 per cent more weight than premature infants who'd received standard medical treatment.

Another study was undertaken by two scientists in the mid-1990s. They travelled to Romania to examine the sensory deprivation of children in understaffed orphanages. They found the touch-deprived children had strikingly lower cortisol and growth development levels for their age group. Due to being starved of touch, they failed to grow to their expected height or weight and showed autistic type characteristics such as lack of eye contact and poor communication skills as well as behavioural problems. So, to say human touch is important is an understatement. According to research, for some it is vital for their existence. In fact, you could say it's actually part of our makeup and something we all desire.

Human touch

Human touch is an extremely undervalued aspect of human nature and has so many healing benefits. It's seen as a sign of respect, acknowledgement or friendliness. Since COVID-19 has entered our world, we are required to keep our distance because getting too close to someone carries the risk of contracting the virus. Because of this, we've had to change the way we interact with each other and the common greetings of a handshake, a hug or a kiss are now taboo and social distancing is at present a government requirement.

Not being able to have skin-to-skin contact, and social distancing, makes for challenging times, especially for those of us who are tactile people. The media announcements are all about how social distancing and isolation will save lives but it will also create mental health issues. The power of touch has a soothing effect, which triggers an increase of oxytocin (feel good hormone) that reduces stress, lowers cortisol and increases our sense of trust and security. Emotionally, a comforting hand squeeze, a gentle tap on the back, touch on the shoulder, or a reassuring hug can help with stress management. For example, in nursing homes, tactile stimulation and a caring touch are utilised to give patients a sense of wellbeing, comfort and security. Sadly, in this COVID-19 predicament, these are the people who are struggling the most from isolation and the lack of touch. I understand that it's absolutely necessary to have safety procedures in place that will save lives but it does highlight how detrimental the lack of human touch can be to our health.

During this time, many people have lost loved ones and, if they were lucky enough to have a funeral, there were only a small number of people allowed to attend because of the social distancing protocol. How hard must that be to have someone you love pass away yet not be allowed to receive a consoling hug, comforting hand shake or calming touch from those who are dear? It's times like these that highlight how much benefit a simple touch can be for your wellbeing.

Whether you're a tactile person or not, human touch and connection are important for our existence and, although you may be OK with the solitude or having no contact, I'm sure your mental and physical wellbeing would benefit greatly from even small connections.

Put that phone away

I find it interesting how we know and understand the importance of connection yet when we get the opportunity to experience it, we behave so differently. I'll admit that I'm a people watcher. I can sit for hours just observing people, how they interact and behave. It fascinates me. I just love it!

How often have you seen a group of friends together and most of them have their head in their electronic devices, not even interacting? It's ironic that people would make the effort to physically meet up yet find it more stimulating or important to be on their devices than being present.

Recently, while on holidays, I couldn't help noticing how attached some people were to their devices. They're constantly on their phone, whether it's sending messages, scrolling, posting on social media. It's quite bizarre that people can be on holidays, at the beach, catching up with friends or family, yet never fully connect with the company they're with. For example, I was watching a group of four people having a meal in a restaurant and, at one stage, all four were on their phones, none of them interacting with each other. I'm sure they believed they were catching up with each other even though, to me, it seemed they weren't connecting. People talk about connecting and building healthy relationships yet sabotage their efforts by not being present. Constant distraction causes us to lose focus, although some people would argue that they're good multi-taskers and believe they're still being present, but the reality is, their mind is distracted so they miss the moment. There will come a time when those catch-ups and special moments aren't around anymore and all the tweets, posts and selfies won't bring them back. I'm not against using electronic devices but when you are connecting face-to-face, put your phone away, be present and give the people you're with the attention they deserve. It's a sign of respect and that you care.

Let's hope the human touch is never replaced or gets lost through the distance of technology and social media. Our growing preoccupation with electronic communication, combined with the social and legal restrictions over physical contact in schools, workplaces and now, due to COVID-19, social distancing rules, add to this conundrum. It will be a very sad day if technology and social media become the best indicator of how well we communicate and connect.

I seriously hope we never lose the value of the human touch and continue to be physical and present, using eye contact, face-to-face encounters and tactile methods as our main ways to communicate and connect. If we live in a world where human touch becomes less important and is seen as invasive or inappropriate, we're sure to see a huge rise in anxiety, depression, mental health issues, and people suffering from life threatening illnesses.

You might need somethin' to hold on to
When all the answers, they don't amount to much
Somebody that you could just to talk to
And a little of that human touch – **Bruce Springsteen**

How do we connect better?

Technology is becoming increasingly ever-present as one of our main sources of communication. It allows us to connect with anyone, anywhere in the world with a click of a button. This is absolutely amazing and has so many benefits but it's also quite scary. Imagine what it would be like if genuine connection, as in face-to-face contact, ever became insignificant. Imagine if we only connect with people through our electronic devices. I hope we never ever get to experience such a situation and that we continue to practice our physical form of connecting with others.

Another reason why physically connecting with others has diminished is that we've become prisoners of busyness. We pack way too much into our life and therefore leave less time for catching up with others. Have you ever been in the situation where you're in a hurry and a friend calls you and wants to talk and your first reaction is, like, really, not now! Can't this wait? You either chat and cut the conversation short or not be present because of your preoccupation in your own importance. Now think about this, how would you feel if something happened to that person and you never got to chat to, or see them, ever again? I'm thinking you'd feel pretty horrible and be disappointed in yourself for being so selfish and placing your busyness as a higher priority than a chat with a friend. My point? We need to make time for connecting, listening and being present for the people that are important in our world. This doesn't mean we have to respond to their every need but be aware of the importance of connecting and being present because one day that opportunity will be gone. And when it's gone, it's gone!

Life can change in an instant, as I have said, and when you lose someone close, no matter how hard you wish for it, there's no bringing them back. That's why it's important to connect, communicate and tell the people you love, how much you appreciate them. It's such a simple thing to do yet, how often do we do it? If there's any one thing that I'd like you to take from this book, it's make time to communicate and connect with those you love, care for and who add value to your world because one day they may not be there for you to appreciate them.

CHAPTER 6:
Simplicity, Mindset and Having fun

Simplicity

As we progress on our way through life, we go through a process of accumulating stuff, both materialistically and emotionally, some useful and some not so. We collect materialistic things through necessity, and also, for leisure and/or pleasure. Whatever the need over the years, it starts to accrue and if not controlled, can create a massive amount of clutter. And it's only every so often we have a stocktake to assess what we've accumulated and decide to declutter, to sort out what's worth holding onto and what's not. It's in these moments that we decide whether something is a help or hinderance and, depending on the decision, it's either gone for good or just moved to another location.

Decluttering for most of us has a feel-good factor to it, especially if you give your stuff away to a charity or someone who will use and appreciate it. Most times when we mention clutter, we talk about the tangibles, the materialistic things we've bought and now disregard or that no longer serve a purpose. We think of stuff we bought to satisfy a need or a desire and now it has done its job and has become redundant in your world. Now some of those things have been very helpful and served their purpose whereas others have been an impulse buy to keep up with the Joneses, stroke our ego or for an emotional boost, and once the novelty has worn off has been superseded for something new.

There's no doubt it feels good to buy new things, especially when it serves a purpose. I love when I have purchased something that I can utilise and is of great value but you also have to know when the use-by date is and be strong enough to let it go. I have an old lawnmower (it was my dad's) that's very temperamental. I reckon I spend more time pulling it apart and purchasing new parts for it than I do mowing. In fact, it's more of a hinderance than a help. Eventually I may get to mow the lawn and it looks good but the time and effort I've put into it outweighs the satisfaction. In fact, I'd be better getting rid of it and reinvesting my time, effort and money on something more reliable.

It's funny how we can justify the complexity of holding onto something that causes us so much angst with minimal return than making things simple and getting a new one. Emotionally we do this too. We hold onto thoughts, memories and people that give us angst and no longer add value to our lives. We hold onto emotions like the old mower, even though they constantly let us down, cost us our time and leave our emotional garden still full of weeds. Every now and again we need to check in on our emotional clutter and do a stocktake to get rid of what's draining our energy or not serving us well. It's about keeping things simple and learning to manage ourselves better.

I think we've all been through a time when we have held onto emotional baggage or a toxic relationship for way too long hoping things would change, when deep down you knew it was never going to happen. To use the lawnmower analogy, we can be the same with people, some people require lots of maintenance and often let you down especially when most needed, yet we still hang onto them. We allow ourselves to get upset by their inconsistencies and constant let downs yet seldom question why. Although they're energy vampires who drain our energy and cause us emotional grief, we hold onto them as hoping (like the old lawnmower) that one day they'll start up and everything will be good again. Sometimes we need to do an audit on our relationships to see which ones we need to eliminate to create space for better ones. Holding onto things or emotions that require too much maintenance, take up space or no longer serve a purpose, is unwise. The sooner you simplify and eliminate them, the quicker you'll be able to move forward. I know it's not as easy as just culling people or things that no longer serve a purpose but when we become too attached to something/someone that no longer adds value, severing the emotional tie can be the best thing to do. The problem is that we complicate the process because of the emotional attachment where, if we simplify the process by asking the question, *'Does this add value to my life?'*, we would be able to eliminate and declutter accordingly.

You don't need much

Humans are good at giving our hard-earned cash away to buy products we don't need to, most times, impress people who don't care. Most people spend well above their means to satisfy a desire or need they think will make a difference. A large majority of the population love to shop and do so for many reasons. For example, how many times have you bought something, whether you needed it or not, because you thought it was a bargain, was cheap or on special? I'd say most of us, which is OK on the odd occasion, but when we start to buy things to fill a void or make us feel better, the story changes. Everybody loves a bargain and finding one definitely feels good but the reality is that there's forever going to be a price reduction or a special offer going on but some people just can't help themselves because it's a bargain.

The thing is, always chasing a bargain has led us into a society of consumers of shit and, most times, shit we don't need. Just look into any household, garage or wardrobe and I can guarantee you'll see heaps of stuff that has been superseded, has never been used or is just waiting for that special moment that never comes. It doesn't make sense to me why people buy things they don't really need and justify it by saying it was a bargain. It's similar to the cold caller trying to sell their product. I don't need anyone telling me to buy their product because they have a special. If I really wanted it, I'd either have it already or go and get it myself! Thank you!

We need to work out what's necessary, what adds value to our world and stop accumulating junk that we never use. In a sense, when it comes to materialistic things, I'm a bit of a minimalist, where I'll only buy what I need when I need it. Whereas, for others, they feel the more they have the better their life will be. I picked up this habit very early as an adult when I was backpacking and it occurred to me that I can actually get by with the stuff on my back and if I needed anything else to add value to my world then I would purchase it and I have kept the same philosophy ever since. Think about it. We accumulate heaps of stuff that we believe we need to survive our daily grind, yet when we go on holiday, we downsize to fit everything we need into a suitcase and, most times, are OK with it. I know a holiday is a little different but the point is, we get by, we improvise and adapt to the situation and are OK with it therefore proving that we really don't need much to get by on.

Minimalism

Speaking of minimalising and travel, a great example of that is my swiss army knife, I remember when I first got it as a gift and thought, 'Hmmm well, thanks, when the hell am I ever going to use this? Well as it worked out, that knife has become one of my most valuable travel items. The more I travelled, the smarter I had to get with my luggage. The amount of times that knife has come to the rescue is remarkable. I don't need to take lots of different utensils and tools because now I have one small item that requires minimal space and has many purposes.

Growing up in a large family, we didn't have much but what we did have I made good use of and greatly appreciated. I've carried that philosophy throughout my life, therefore don't buy things unless I need or absolutely want them. Some would say this is being lousy, maybe it is, but I'd rather have what I need and spend the rest on travel than have a heap of stuff that only gives me short-term joy.

Being minimalistic is an interesting concept. For some, depending on how fanatical they are about it, it can almost be extremism. They live on the bare essentials in a tiny living space with no or minimal materialistic possessions. That's great if that's what floats your boat but to me minimalism is about keeping it simple, not getting attached to stuff, eliminating the unnecessary and making room for what's of value and significance. I apply this theory in all aspects of my life from relationships, home, work and travel so I can, to use my dad's words, **travel light**.

Over time we can accumulate lots of stuff and much of this I believe, we no longer require yet are too afraid to eliminate because we give meaning to it. We tell ourselves a story of why we need it therefore hold onto it. A perfect example of this is the person who cannot get rid of things even when they are no longer being used. They create a story of why it means so much to them and wonder why they find it hard to let it go. Sentimentality is OK but not if it means you're hoarding or are too afraid to eliminate people or things that no longer serve you or are holding you back.

Holding onto things or having attachment is neither good nor bad but my view is the more stuff you have, the more stuff you have to worry about. When it comes to materialistic needs, being minimalistic helps greatly when making decisions and keeps my life simple.

Complexity

There is strength in simplicity and when it comes to living life, some people make the process harder than it needs to be. We're all different and react differently but the way we react plays a huge part in determining whether we make life simple or complex. I'm sure you know someone or maybe it's you, who, whenever confronted with a situation and a decision needs to be made, they'll stress and catastrophise over it to the point of anxiety. They'll continually overthink and exaggerate the extent of the decision thus creating a story in their head about what disasters might or might not happen.

How often have you been in a situation where someone says they need to speak with you and you automatically go into panic mode. You start thinking about all the negative things it could be about yet when you talk, it was nothing like what you thought in your head. We sometimes make the simple complex with our negative thinking; we waste energy focusing on what could happen rather than how we can manage it. It's not always easy to be calm when making a decision but if our default setting is always reacting poorly whenever we're faced with a dilemma, there's a fair chance things are going to get complicated.

Life is one big decision-making process and the better we get at making decisions, the simpler our life becomes. We can fuss and carry on about how tough life is and spend our time avoiding things but all that does is prolong the process. Somewhere along the way a decision has to be made so you may as well decide and the more you do that the easier it becomes to do it again. As a mentor of mine always tells me, you can't get good at things you never practice so start practicing!

Throughout life we'll make thousands, maybe millions, of decisions and not all of them are going to be great but it's in those decisions where life happens, and you learn about yourself and how to become more efficient. I used to be a great avoider and at times still am. If I didn't have to make a decision or if I could rely on someone else, I would. It took me awhile to realise that relying on someone else was complicated because you have little control over the outcome and the worst part was that some of those decisions took me in a direction I didn't like. Once I decided to be more accountable for my actions, I discovered making my own decisions, whether good or bad, wasn't as hard as I was making it, therefore it was within my control. It took me awhile, but I eventually realised the more control I took, the simpler my life became. I thought because someone appeared to be smarter and more successful, it would be easier just to copy their processes and procedures.

I soon discovered that I needed to be true to myself, follow the path for me, which meant making my own decisions and being accountable to them. I was being lazy and hoping I could achieve some kind of success without having to do the work. I learned my approach wasn't working so I had to simplify how I went about things. I had to make the process of treading my path to success simple, doable and aligned with my values. I continue to use these processes because they've kept me accountable and on track. Here are a few examples of how simplicity works for me now:

1. Don't try to do too much

When I changed my career direction, I had to gain some qualifications, which meant a lot of studying and learning. This venture into the new landscape of study was exciting. I loved the learning and, due to my newly found passion, I started to become almost obsessed with learning new things but this enthusiasm created a monster. I wanted to know everything and know it now! I thought the more I knew the better I'd become so I enrolled in way too many courses which, in the end, overwhelmed me and made the learning process harder than it needed to be. I realised it's great to be keen and have a passion for learning but it's also smart to know you're learning threshold and be disciplined enough to work within it. The lesson—know your limits, focus on a few things and do them well!

2. Have procedures

I like to be structured and organised but without being obsessive. One area where I find this habit awesome is travel. I love my travel and whenever I do get the chance, I want it to be as stress free as possible. To do that I have lists for all the things I need to do prior to the trip, from what to pack and what to take on the plane, to the return home. This helps reduce the stress and worry of forgetting to do something or of leaving something behind. Knowing all the boxes have been ticked, I can relax because I'm not worrying about what hasn't been done and this gets me into holiday mode much quicker.

3. Be real

Trying to be someone or something you're not is hard work. Yes, it's great to have people to aspire too but if that means you're trying to be someone or something you're not, the chances of either burning out or being seen as artificial will increase. Keep it simple. Just be yourself. It's so much easier because once you start being true to yourself, people see you as genuine, which increases your confidence and wastes less time worrying about what others think.

4. Take time out

The Dutch have a lifestyle concept called Niksen—the art of doing nothing. Learn to be OK with taking time out to do not much. Being productive and getting things done is fantastic but if you're always caught up in the busyness of life and trying to be productive, your effectiveness actually reduces. I learned that allowing myself to stop for a while to just sit and do nothing, or very little, my energy, creativity and problem-solving ability increased. Being constantly busy means your body is always running on adrenaline, which is tiring and can impact your health, causing insomnia, high blood pressure and supressed immune system. Listen to your body and take some time to recharge that body of yours and it'll thank you for it.

Choices

We all have the freedom to choose whatever we want to do, be or have. For some, that's awesome but for others, it's a nightmare. How you perceive that freedom can make the process simple or hard. As we go about our daily routines, we're constantly making choices—from the moment we wake we're deciding whether to get up, press the snooze button, have a shower, go to work, what we should wear, eat, drink—the list goes on. It's endless. We're unconsciously making those choices based on our beliefs, cognitive biases, values, family, peers, wanting to gain approval, past experiences, and most of all, pleasure and pain. There are so many factors that influence our choices, but pleasure or pain are the overriding influencers and most times, depending on its emotional pull, this is how we decide in the end.

I grew up in a very staunch Catholic family and our beliefs and values were based on the bible and the teachings of the Catholic Church. To me, it seemed choice was based on guilt and sin and if I chose what was considered wrong, I'd be punished. For example, simple things like enjoying a big meal was being greedy, having amorous thought about a girl was being impure, cursing someone or something was sinning, etc, etc. So, it seemed every choice was tinged with some form of guilt, which worked for some decisions but not many. I can't help thinking back on how life was like the lyrics of a Travis song, 'Why does it always rain on me, was it because I lied when I was seventeen?', which made making choices difficult. As I grew up and started to form my own opinions, I began to realise how my choices were being dictated by this default setting. It got to a point where even when I was celebrating my accomplishments with a reward, I still felt guilty because I felt I was being self-indulgent. WTF? Whoops, now I feel bad for swearing ☺.

My default belief system was ruling my decision making therefore I was putting unnecessary pressure on myself, which made choice more complex than it needed to be. Eventually I moved on from Catholicism and started to think freely for myself which I might add, wasn't easy. I still find it hard at times, even though I haven't been a practicing Catholic for over 20 years. I often get the guilts about things that I know are totally OK. Our choices, whether good or bad, can always be manipulated by some kind of external influence but if your choices are aligned with your values, the process is so much simpler. We can waste far too much time overthinking and catastrophising over our decisions when if we go on gut feelings, most times the choice will be right.

We all know the feeling when something doesn't resonate with you. You have a gut feeling that something just isn't quite right. I remember a time when I went against this feeling and later wished I hadn't. It was back in my school days when we were on a retreat—a spiritual, come religious, self-awareness type of set up. These retreats went for about 3–4 days and a group of boys who played football decided to go for a run because we were going to miss out on training that week. We went for that run with great intentions but that soon changed as we approached town and the boys decided on buying some beer. Now I wasn't a drinker so, at first, I said no for a few reasons. One was because I didn't even like beer. Another reason was that I didn't want to get into trouble and, most importantly, my gut was telling me this was a dumb idea. Even though it didn't feel right, and my gut was telling me so, I weakened and was eventually persuaded to go with the mob because of the 'one in all in' rule. As one member put it, 'What are the chances of being caught?' We got those beers and hid down a laneway, supposedly out of sight. Well, wouldn't you know it, as soon as I opened that can of beer, the teacher's car pulls into the laneway. Yes, we were caught red handed! The can of beer was in my hand and the teacher eyeballed me. We were guilty! I was so annoyed with myself because I'd realised what a stupid move it was to go against my gut because now, I'm in a lot of trouble not just from the school but, worst of all, from my dad. I can say it was the longest trip home from the retreat that day. What was a half hour journey seemed like an eternity and, as each minute passed, my fears and anxiety grew. I was absolutely shitting myself thinking about what lay ahead. I knew I was in trouble but how much was the concern. In the end, it wasn't as bad as I anticipated but I did get a week's suspension from school and failed religion that term. Now this wasn't anything too disastrous, but my gut was telling me what the best choice was, yet, because of peer pressure, I didn't listen. We all have a good laugh about it now, but it was from that moment on I decided to be more aware of my gut feelings when making decisions. These days I try to keep the choice-making process simple. I base my decisions on what aligns with my values and listening to my gut instincts.

Mindset

Have you ever wondered why you think, act and respond the way you do or why some things annoy the hell out of you, where others don't? It's all to do with your mindset, your thoughts, beliefs and the influences you've collected over the years that have shaped your view of the world. Your mindset affects the way you see and make sense of things, it's the information we base our decisions and direction on. Our mindset is our default setting that goes deep into our core. It's the belief system we use to identify who we are and what we stand for and it can be the maker or breaker of how we navigate life. Your mindset is an accumulation of years and years of thoughts, experiences and influences and, depending on whether they're good or bad ones, will determine the type of thinking you own. How you think, respond and act is in a sense controlled by your mindset. Mindset is a massive area that has so many factors that influence it and for me to cover it scientifically wouldn't do it justice so I will leave that up to the scientist.

Saying that, I think mindset is a huge factor when it comes to finding significance so I will talk about it from my perspective and experiences. I believe our thinking is vital in how we approach life. Our thinking is what influences our decisions, what we're grateful for, who we connect with and how complex or simple we make it. Our mindset, although deep-seated, can be influenced by external factors which can change how we think. Using my own experience, I believe my mindset has influenced my behavior and often held me back from creating something better.

What influences our mindset

Mindset is the way we think, organise and orientate our way through life. Our mindset dictates the actions we take, how we think and go about them. Our mindset is formed through a combination of our thoughts, experiences and values and it's those influences that determine the way we view the world. According to psychologist Carol Dweck, there are two types of mindset—fixed and growth. A person with a fixed mindset believes their traits are set and cannot be changed whereas a person with a growth mindset believes that their traits can change through learning and experiences over time.

There are so many influencing factors that determine the type of mindset you develop and the path you walk in life. Influences like friends, family, associates, career, hobbies, likes, dislikes, etc have an effect on our mindset. Let's face it, our mindset is a combination of pretty much everything we've been taught, do, see, hear, desire, believe in and react to. These determining factors influence us from the moment we're born and continue throughout life.

Mindset is pretty much your belief system. For example, people with a fixed mindset will be more reluctant to change and will react and do things a certain way, often without questioning whether it's right or can be done another way. They're quite set in their ways and beliefs, therefore often see things as limited and often negative, whereas the growth mindset person bases their world on learning and experiencing things to increase their chances of creating something better. Now I'm not going to go into the argument of which one is better because that is a massive argument. What I want to talk about is how and why we think the way we do. When it comes to our mindset, the influences we choose will reflect the path we tread. That path is made up of many factors and I will show you why the choices we make are significant.

Firstly, most of our set beliefs are based on our upbringing and events that shape our early lives, like what our parents taught us and what religion, culture or creed we grew up in, and these are hard to change. These are hardwired in us until we learn to think for ourselves. You are totally influenced by them and it is therefore hard for you to question whether they are right or wrong. As I said earlier, I grew up in a very strict Catholic household and, while under that roof, I was taught not to question but to do what was expected of me. It's through those teachings I developed my sense of good and bad, which became my mindset at the time. As I was growing up, there were many other events and occurrences that helped shape my mindset. Things like the sayings and phrases my parents used such as, 'Don't go out in the rain, you'll catch a cold', 'Pride comes before a fall', 'Everything happens for a reason', 'Time heals all wounds', 'Eat your crusts and you'll get curly hair', 'What doesn't kill you makes you stronger', or 'Eating carrots helps you see better in the dark.' So many times, I heard these sayings and just believed them without asking why or questioning the proof behind them, and some of them are still ingrained in my head.

As the years rolled on and I started to experience life my own way, I started to question these beliefs, which changed the way I viewed life. This has enabled me to be more open-minded, react more rationally, to learn from others and make better decisions based on my own set of beliefs. Looking back, I still hold onto some of these, but my mindset is one that works on a different thought pattern, which resonates with *my* values and not that of a child's fixed mindset. My parents, at the time, influenced my mindset and, like most kids, I adored them so why would I ever need to question them?

Other influences come from the people we associate with: friends, family, peers, and groups. Each of these tend to play a huge part in how we think and operate but being able to listen and learn yet still be strong enough to make up your own mind, shows that we are willing to grow and expand our mindset. There have been many times I've been at a party or at a dinner where someone starts sprouting off about their chosen topic with such conviction that I take what was being said as fact. Later I have used that information only to be told it wasn't entirely true. I realised I was being influenced more by their confidence so, without questioning the information, I let it become a belief.

When you admire, look up to, or respect someone, often they'll influence your thinking and behaviour for both good and bad. Have you ever experienced someone change their behaviour when in a group or around certain people? I had a friend who was awesome company yet when in a certain group, changed dramatically. One on one we'd have wonderful conversations and share personal stories and just be comfortable with each other, yet as soon as he was in a group or with certain people, he'd change. It was as if we hardly knew each other. It's OK to have people you admire and want to emulate but never lose who you are just to be liked or gain approval.

I think most of the time we're influenced by our feelings, emotions and desires and, depending on how strongly they're pulling on our heart strings, they become a huge part of our mindset. We are emotional beings and the way we think, act and feel is hugely influenced by how we are brought up. What do I mean by that? The religion, philosophy, culture, politics, music, books, lessons, rules, traditions, and behaviours we learned or were taught become the foundations for who we are. These influences remain with us throughout life although they may change over time. Generally, they're deep-seated and, as much as we try to deny it, it's often those deep-seated emotions that dictate our thinking. I often have this experience where someone will say something negative about Catholics which I agree with, yet my initial gut reaction is to react with a subconscious, 'Be careful' and then settle and listen. This type of deep-seated belief is the hardest to rid yourself of (or is it that bloody Catholic guilt thing again?). Even though they no longer serve you, these emotional attachments can still be strong.

Emotional attachments can be so strong that they become such a strong part of our mindset that we seldom question them until something happens that rocks our world. The belief system we developed from a young age soon becomes our hard-wired default setting and the influence for our language and behaviour, which may not always serve us well.

We all have the ability to be free-thinking but we also need to be aware of how others think. We can only do this when we question our own beliefs to see where they come from. In doing so we can see whether they're serving or sabotaging us because sometimes the beliefs we hold onto limit our progress, keeping us trapped in a mindset that becomes harder and harder to get out of. As a young lad growing up in a small country town, I had a lot of habits and behaviours and never questioned my beliefs, and it wasn't until I travelled and experienced life outside of my bubble that my eyes were opened to the awareness of how differently other people think. By the way, regardless of where you grow up, we all tend to live in our own bubble. I loved growing up in the country and had some wonderful experiences and great lessons but, over that time, I also developed some limiting beliefs that, for years, held me back from exploring my potential. These limiting beliefs were a by-product of the years of influences from my family, friends, religion, and the cultural environment I lived in.

For years and years, I held the belief that city people were selfish, nasty and stuck up, so I avoided going to the city and would be dammed if I was ever going to live there. Well, as time passed on, those limiting beliefs were challenged and, through those challenges, I discovered people are pretty much the same no matter where you live. My beliefs were created by people who were never destined to live in the city, which is fine, but for me it became the place where my life changed for the better. It was the place where I started my business, met some amazing friends and associates, and married my wife. Now if I never questioned my limited beliefs about the city and let the old default mindset influence my decision, I wouldn't have the experiences and awesome life I have now. The lyrics to the John Mellencamp song, 'Small Town' always resonate with me:

Well I was born in a small town
And I can breathe in a small town
Gonna die in this small town
And that's probably where they'll bury me.

This is because that was my belief. I had no intentions of living in the city. I didn't think I had many options. It was like I was living to the lines of the Springsteen song, 'The River'…'I *come from down in the valley where, mister, when you're young, they bring you up to do like your daddy done'.* I was destined to do the same unless something changed. I had to question my beliefs, which was extremely difficult at the time. You know the situation; you're doing what's expected of you without questioning the reasons why.

The significance of the story is: I worked in a job I didn't like for over twelve years until I hit my boiling point where the frustration and the feeling of being stuck was too much. I badly wanted change to happen yet was too afraid to do it. I knew my beliefs were holding me back, but the thought of change was daunting. I had yet to question my beliefs and it wasn't until I did that, I realised how much my emotions and feelings were influencing my decisions and limiting my potential. We need to be aware how much our mindset can be limiting our progress and be brave enough to question their origins to decide whether they're a barrier or a benefit.

I believe we can float between a fixed and growth mindset where they're both working together simultaneously. From my own experience, there are times when I can be very fixed in my thinking and be reluctant to change whereas other times, I can be open to learning and adaptable to experiencing other points of view. I think we flow in and out of each mindset and which one we use at any given time, depends on what's happening around us and our attitude towards that external influence. So, to say someone has either a fixed or a growth mindset, is more blurred than that.

Attitude plays a huge role in how we perceive a person, place or thing. You know the analogy of the glass half full or half empty and which one you are. To a certain degree that works. Let's break that down a little. The glass half empty person is supposedly the negative thinker and sees the problem rather than the solution and, in most situations, is a pessimist. You know the type, always complaining how unfair and tough life is. Then there's the glass half full person. They're the positive ones who sees the possibility, not the problem. They look at life as an opportunity to grow. They are the optimist.

Most of us want to believe we're the glass half full person because it makes us feel better about ourselves but, if the truth be known, we're actually somewhere in the middle and the judgement of the glass lies with our attitude. I know people will disagree with me because they'll say the pessimist looks for the negative in a situation and that's not me but I think it's a human instinct to naturally look for the negatives before seeing the positives. My point is, when we are confronted with a challenge or problem, we instantly think the worst then it depends on our attitude at the time whether or not we respond positively. In the heat of the moment, our first thoughts are WTF? then it'll fluctuate between positive and negative and that's when we allow our attitude to come off the bench and take control of the game.

You can argue attitude and mindset are the same thing and, to a certain degree, you're right. The difference, I believe, is that mindset is your subconscious thoughts that have been formed over a period of time and become the foundation of your thinking whereas attitude is your thinking at the time of the event, which can be affected by the external influences. Take for example, in a group, someone says something that really pisses you off yet no one else sees it as a problem. Your first reaction is to argue with them because your mindset believes it's wrong and you're offended. You then look around to see no one else cares, if they don't, you change your approach, smile or even nervously laugh it off and pretend you're OK. What has happened here is your mindset thinking has reacted instantly but then, because of the external influences, your attitude (or how you hope to be seen) kicks in to help control your behaviour and adapt to suit the situation.

Attitude is what you want people to see whereas mindset is what you actually think. Your attitude can make or break you in an instance because it's seen, whereas mindset is a learned behaviour that isn't as easily picked up in a situation. We can mask our attitude for good and bad, like the example above. If I want someone to think I have a positive attitude, all I have to do is pretend to smile and say positive things and people think I'm a great bloke. It's a bit like social media. It's easy to write or post things that look exciting, cool, funny, flattering, or even romantic to impress others but most times it's not who we really are. Anyone can put on the attitude mask of positivity, niceness and charm to impress, yet when no one's looking, they're a completely different person. Attitude can be a great tool to hide behind; the facade that hides the real you.

Although attitude can be situational, most times, we refer to attitude as someone's demeanour. We say things like they have a great or shitty attitude or they're so positive/negative when speaking about someone. We love labelling people and depending on their label, we decide whether or not we will associate with them. Let's face it, if you had to choose who you hang with, you're going to pick people with a good attitude. Going back to the half full or half empty glass analogy, think of attitude as the tap that fills your glass and, if yours needs filling, get water from a tap that flows rather than one that's blocked.

Attitude is a choice and that choice can be the difference between having a good or a bad day. The minute you wake up, you have a choice about your attitude and that is an important determinant on how the rest of your day will pan out. You get to choose your attitude and that choice plays a significant role in influencing the type of outcomes you encounter.

Attitude is important when it comes to finding significance. It's the good and bad, the happy and sad, the confidence or fear, the calm or the chaos, the yin and yang. It's the driver of our behaviour. Attitude becomes the determinant of how our life unfolds. It becomes the piece in the jigsaw puzzle of life that helps people perceive, accept and connect with us. It's a social concept that we use to decide what a person is like and that decision determines whether doors will be opened or shut on you. For example, someone with a good attitude has a better chance of being let through the door than someone whose attitude stinks. I remember in the early days of my business I used to spend a lot of time and money on coaches and mentors trying to help me build my business. I recall a situation where business was struggling, and things weren't moving as I had hoped. My meetings with my business coach were very negative due to my poor attitude at the time. I would enter the meetings with all this negative energy and talk about all the things that were going wrong, never mentioning the positive things that were happening, I'd focus on the negative and my attitude portrayed the same story. I had the 'woe-is-me' attitude yet somehow was expecting my coach to wave the magic wand and make it all better. I remember thinking how shitty this whole business thing was and wondering why I should continue. During a run (I do my best thinking while running) I wondered if I changed my approach/attitude and just spoke about the positive things that were happening in our next meeting, would it change anything? To my surprise, it changed everything—from the words we used, to the action we took. There was a real energy, a positive vibe, so to speak, which took the coaching session to a new level. The bizarre thing was, nothing had changed in my world except my attitude towards it but that was enough to create the momentum to help change the trajectory of where I was heading. Now I'm not saying change your attitude and your world automatically becomes awesome. Far from it. It takes a lot of hard work but by adopting a better attitude, the chances of doors opening increases.

Self-doubt

Self-doubt is a confidence killer and can mess with your head. It has the power to make you start questioning your own ability which, if not controlled, can manifest into a belief. You're thinking plays a major role in the way you react. For example, when things go wrong, we can either view it as a catastrophe or a challenge. We all react differently to different situations. Some people will react badly and fall into the 'woe-is-me' syndrome. They see the situation as a catastrophe and let the event become their main focus, whereas for others, even though they've confronted with exactly the same event, they see it as an opportunity to learn from or try something new.

Whenever things aren't going to plan, it's easy to let your emotions take control and if your default setting is self-doubt, your emotions can quickly turn a trivial mishap into a major drama. In most situations, there's usually an underlying message being relayed and if we listen to the message, it's often a sign or a signal for us to either change our thinking about what's occurring or how we proceed. In all the mayhem that's occurring, we need to control our thoughts to gain some clarity to enable us to make better decisions. Sometimes, amid all the chaos and self-doubt, this may be easier said than done but it's exactly what's needed.

I remember one day at school when I was mucking up in class and the teacher said to me, 'The way you're going, you'll amount to nothing, McAllister.' Sadly, as much as I laughed it off at the time, due to my lack of confidence, a lot of what he said stuck with me. For a long time afterwards, every time I failed, or something went wrong, I'd subconsciously repeat those words in my head, telling myself he was right. The thing is, maybe part of what he said was true because I'll admit that I could be a bit of a shit at times but to say I'd amount to nothing was quite destructive. As the years progressed, I had to realise that throughout life, people will say all types of shit to you from encouragement to cruelty and it's your self-belief that'll be the difference to how it affects you.

Years later, as I ponder that moment at school, in hindsight, it altered my opinion of myself and I let it become my belief. I would avoid, make excuses or only half-try at things just in case I wasn't good enough or might fail. How often do we avoid what's hard or requires a bit of effort because our self-doubt kicks in? For most of my adult life, I would only attempt things I was good at to avoid failure or being criticised until I realised how much this was holding me back. I wanted to do different things, better things, yet kept putting them off and it got to a point where my self-doubt was controlling my life and I had to decide—Do I keep kidding myself by wearing my poorly fitting confidence coat or back myself in and start wearing one that fits?

The thing is, we can appear shiny and new on the outside but inside is a totally different story. This apprehension was continuously playing with my head. Self-doubt was knocking at the door and my negative self-talk was welcoming it with open arms. Somewhere amongst all this mental angst I had to change my thinking and be accountable because the only person who could make the change was **me**!

How many times does this happen? We keep putting things off due to fear, discomfort or self-doubt, only to discover that when we do commit, it wasn't as bad as we thought.

I notice this happens a lot when people are attempting to get into shape. They procrastinate, find excuses and avoid starting because it's all too hard or they might fail. Getting into shape isn't easy but if we are forever using our fears and doubts as a reason for not trying, we're never going to know what's possible. It's like most things in life, if you want to create a change for the better, you have to do the work. Change doesn't happen just because you thought about it, change comes about through action. I know this sounds like motivational speak but the reality is, unless you have a crack at something, how can you ever know what you're capable of? I had to get real with myself and if I ever wanted to overcome my self-doubt, I had to confront my demons. This was bloody scary and continuous hard work but over time, with quite a few failures (or shall we call them lessons), I'm managing them better. I'm still a work in progress and those self-doubt demons still appear, especially when I make mistakes, but these days I'm OK with that.

Too often people stop pursuing what they want because it's hard work. They subconsciously beat themselves up about whether they're good enough or not, reinforcing the doubts and fears already in place. It's amazing how the mind works! You can be going along so well but at the first sign of difficulty, the subconscious mind kicks in and creates doubt around your capabilities.

We need to understand that our feelings of fear, anxiety and making mistakes are part of the journey. If we constantly beat ourselves up whenever things don't go to plan, our chances of success diminish and self-doubt increases. It's about having belief in our own ability and reducing the doubt of whether we're good enough and understanding that even though we'll make mistakes and struggle with self-doubt, that's OK. We're all a work in progress. No one's perfect and even though some people appear to wear the confidence coat so well, I can bet on some level that coat gets uncomfortable and they battle with self-doubt.

Fears and worry

Another area where our mindset determines our outcomes is fear and worry. We all have a built-in radar called the sympathetic nervous system, commonly referred to as the fight or flight response. This is the fear response system and it kicks in whenever we encounter any threat or danger. It gets activated whenever we are confronted or frightened by someone or something. The body instantly releases hormones that react to that stimulus and, in that moment, like The Clash song, you decide, 'Should I stay or should I go?' Fear is a feeling or reaction to a perception of danger and is an internal warning system to keep us safe.

Worry, on the other hand, is thinking about future events or threats that create anxiety, stress or apprehension. Worry is based on how we think something will turn out or thinking ahead about something that might not happen. Worry is where overthinking blurs the lines between the hypothetical and reality. It's where we attempt to solve future events mentally using hypotheticals to predict an outcome which most times is uncertain. Worry is the fight or flight response put on steroids. It's where thinking about something that hasn't even happened causes it to grow and become more credible than it should be.

Whether you're a worrier or not, fear and worry are interlinked and at some stage we'll all encounter some form of both. That's not a bad thing. In fact, it can work in your favour to keep you safe or help you to make better decisions. Think of a time when you were walking in the dark or you were home alone and you started to hear footsteps behind you, or noises outside, and instantly your gut started churning. That's definitely fear and worry but it's good because it alerted your senses and you've become aware of your surroundings, so you started planning accordingly. This type of worry is short-term and is about self-preservation and decision making and that's healthy, but when that fear or worry becomes part of your everyday thinking, where you're always seeing danger and you procrastinate, that's an obstructive mindset.

Anxiety is so prevalent these days and is one of the major influences why people are so afraid to be or create differently. Everyone wants to be different yet deep down we're often too afraid to step into that space. Looking back on my youth, I was so scared of being rejected, ostracised or failing that I would follow the pack just to fit in even when it felt wrong. I would worry about so many things like looking dumb, being poor, my looks, my beliefs, my family, even how long I'd be on this planet. I distinctly remember when I was about seven years old and Mum took us to an aged care home to visit some elderly people and there were some who looked like death warmed up. It absolutely scared the hell out of me. For many weeks later, I would lie in bed at night too afraid to go to sleep because I didn't want to get old or die! My fears and worries about getting old and dying became my reality and caused me a lot of worry, which today would be diagnosed as anxiety. I let my hypothetical thinking and fear override my reality and stop me from doing things that I believed could cause me harm or make me old. Let's jump forward fifty years. Thank goodness I controlled my thinking around that because firstly, I'm still alive and have done many great (and even some dangerous) things and secondly, they haven't made me old nor killed me yet!

We let fear and worry stop us from stepping out of our comfort zone to try new or different things. We do this because we worry about what may or may not happen. We worry about so many things, thinking we're the only ones with that issue. We somehow believe we're unique, that 'no one else is like me' yet in some form we all fear and worry about the 'would'ves, should'ves and could'ves'. We all, to some extent fear failure, success, love, rejection, looking dumb, being inadequate, change, uncertainty, missing out, being judged, things going wrong, the list goes on and the reality is we all do it. So what??

Fear and worry are a part of the human experience and unless we're aware of its potential, we can let it inhibit rather than enhance us. It obstructs our internal radar system and blocks our spatial awareness, our attunement and gut instincts that help us determine which direction to travel or which decisions to make. The thing is: we're all going through similar experiences, just at different levels. We all struggle with what others are thinking about us and the sooner we realise that, the easier it will be to grasp the idea that no one gives a shit because they're usually too busy worrying about their own shit to be concerned about yours. That's actually good because once you can drop the 'everyone is watching me' thinking, the simpler life becomes. We spend way too much time living in our heads, thinking about what others are thinking of us, which is time consuming, energy zapping and just not worth it.

Our mindset is powerful and when controlled in a productive way, it enhances our progress and allows us to be the architect of wonderful experiences. I believe doubt, fear and worry are things we must go through to understand our thinking and it's those experiences that help shape who we are and how we act and react. It's being able to understand yourself enough to know that you will make mistakes and that things will go wrong. So what? Learning from your mistakes allows you to be true to yourself, to learn and to be grateful for the opportunity to gain wisdom through experience. Recognising our mindset allows us to connect, be loved, build friendships, and share our problems. It helps reduce the anxiety and pressure we put on ourselves and makes life simpler.

Having fun

When will we ever be happy?

According to the Australian Bureau of Statistics, 1 in 5 Australians suffer from some sort of mental health issue (depression, anxiety, self-harm, suicide). This is quite an alarming statistic considering one of the most important goals in life is to be happy. I hear people say it all the time, 'I will be happy when I lose 5 kgs', 'fit into my favourite jeans', 'meet the partner of my dreams', 'become more financially secure', 'own my own house', etc yet they spend the whole time stressing about it. Will that bring them happiness? You know, most times I doubt it. I can say this from experience because when they do reach their goal, it just becomes another piece in their jigsaw of chasing eternal happiness so it soon loses its appeal or is superseded by the next big thing.

Are we trying so hard to find happiness that it's creating stress and anxiety?

Maybe we need to simplify what happiness really is. There seems to be a lot of unnecessary demands around being happy. The self-help industry plays into this by selling the dream with statements like, *'Don't worry be happy!'*, *'Smile and everything will be ok'*, or *'Just think positively and it'll work out.'* These statements are great in theory but tell that to someone who's just lost their lifelong partner or has gone through some major trauma and see if it resonates. It's not as if you can just turn on the happiness switch and all is fun again. I think it's these types of messages that, although meant to be positive, are adding unnecessary pressure around happiness and thus contributing to the mental health statistics.

It's ironic that for some, the pursuit of happiness is the very thing that's causing stress and anxiety.

There's a belief today we should be happy all the time and if not, there's something wrong and we need fixing. According to the dictionary, happiness *is 'an* emotional *or effective state that is characterised by feelings of enjoyment and satisfaction.'* If happiness is an emotional state, that means it can change at any time, so thinking you should always be happy is not only being delusional, it's absurd. The reality is: you won't be happy all the time and thinking so will only lead to disappointment. You're going to experience periods of grief and sadness throughout life and anyone who thinks otherwise is kidding themselves.

I believe the issue is that we yearn for happiness yet struggle defining it. People often chase an idea of what they think happiness might be, like a bigger house, better job, more money, a flash car, a better body... (insert your wish here), only to realise it hasn't produced the 'happily-ever-after' dream they hoped for. They're looking externally for things they perceive will bring happiness rather than looking internally for true meaning and purpose in life.

If our happiness is entrenched in something external, it can be taken away from us at any time so there will always be the chance of disappointment, loss and uncertainty. How many times have you wanted something so badly that you could hardly wait yet when you got it, the anticipation just didn't live up to expectation? We hope when it happens that our world will change for the better and we'll be eternally happy. In theory, that's what makes the juice worth the squeeze.

I'm not implying that happiness is this unachievable Holy Grail that is out of reach but it's also not something that is with us all the time. Finding happiness is definitely achievable but we need to understand it's not permanent. It's an emotion and our emotions are constantly changing to suit whatever stimulus we're facing at the time. The goal of wanting to be happy all the time is a massive ask, especially when there are so many factors we can't control. It's like eating an ice cream in the midday sun and expecting it not to melt.

Happiness is a choice and how you choose to be happy is personal. You can choose simplicity and be happy with who you are and with what you have and do in life, or you can keep chasing the next big thing, hoping that'll bring you happiness. We need to accept that happiness, like ice cream, will have its pleasurable moments as well as its melting ones. The key is trying to keep the disappointment to a minimum and to achieve that, perhaps we should be looking at happiness from a different perspective.

If we simplify things a little and don't take ourselves so seriously, if we learn to laugh at ourselves, enjoy, appreciate and be grateful for the little things that happen in our life, we will see happiness in small things. Simple things can bring so much pleasure, like watching your kids playing, spending quality time with your partner, going for a walk along the beach, listening to your favourite music, laughing with friends, and having fun. You know what I'm talking about. Sadly, too often we take these occasions for granted and the appreciation of their value is lost.

I think, as a society, we've become way too serious. We like to think we are easy going and fun to be around but forget to remove the serious mask when attempting to have fun. Have you ever been to a dinner or a party where everyone is caught up in their own importance, pretending to be sophisticated or appear smart? It's annoying! Drop the façade and just be you and, dare I say it, have some fun!

I must admit, in my early years of running a business, that was me. I thought to be successful you had to be serious, which was hard work. I would put on the business persona of being serious to impress people using terms and phrases that quite frankly were a wank and looking back, so was I. I would frown when employees were having too much fun or being silly because business is serious stuff and they obviously weren't taking their job seriously. I wanted to show people (terms I used back then) how I was on top of my game, giving 110%, and ready to take the business to the next level. WTF? I must have been a pain in the arse! The funny thing was that it didn't make me or the business look any smarter. Looking back, I realised being too serious didn't allow me to enjoy the process and all that did was create angst and make the business a dull place to work.

These days, thank goodness, I've relaxed and like to enjoy what I do and have some fun while I do it. I'm a person who likes to have a laugh, but I stopped being that person because I took myself way too seriously! Not that I go around forever laughing but I like to see the lighter side of life because, let's face it, at times life can be pretty screwed up. We spend a huge amount of our life at work so why not make it as enjoyable and fun as possible?

We need to just chill a little and have some fun. The world has become a place full of gloom and doom, where you have to be careful what you say and do because it might offend someone. Yes, there is a time and a place for everything, but to not be able to laugh at yourself or things that happen because someone else may get offended, is restrictive. When you look at life from a humorous perspective, it's quite comical. We all make mistakes and do dumb shit. So what? It's in those moments that you need to step back and see the funny side of what's happening. Too often we see mistakes as a failure and berate ourselves for the mishap when, most times, if we look at the humorous side of it, we can have a laugh, pick ourself back up again and learn from it. We hate looking silly and somehow want our world to be perfect. This is putting unnecessary pressure on ourselves to perform. I believe this type of thinking has created a seriousness around the way we approach life, where we've become very judgemental and critical of ourselves and others. The pressure to be politically correct, woke or across everything so we don't look stupid or offend, is forever increasing. We have limited our freedom of speech and opinions and in the process, we have lost the fun side of what we're doing and have started to take life too seriously. I totally get that we needed to change and that's been brilliant but to be so scared of saying or doing things because it may offend is making us far too serious. Yes, we need to have awareness of what we say and how we behave so we don't cause harm to others, but we don't need to become so rigid that it stops us having fun.

Life can be tough and sometimes even harsh and to make a go of it you have to work hard. I watched my parents work hard all their lives. They did what they had to do with what they had. To me, it seemed all they did was toil away at life without too much fun. I might have been wrong but as I watched my parents getting older and life pass them by, I started to think, there has to be more to life than just toiling away day after day like some kind of Groundhog Day and then you die. There has to be something better than this, something that makes life more interesting, more purposeful and enjoyable. The thought of following in the path of Mum and Dad was frightening to me and that thought was a catalyst enough for me to have a stocktake on my life, to see what's giving me joy and what's not. That exercise alone is well worth doing, it makes you dig deep into who and what in your life brings you happiness and fun. After my Groundhog Day stocktake, I made a pact with myself to get more out of life, to have more fun. So, I did it my way – I kept it simple!

I wasn't going to turn my life upside down or do anything radical because that's not who I am but what I did was decide to not take life or myself too seriously and have more fun. How I did this was to simplify my life by eliminating the things that were complicating it and use my time on what I enjoyed doing. I decided if that's what I wanted; the only person who can make that happen was me. It was time to stop the bullshit talk, step out of the theory and make it happen. From that moment on, I was about not taking life so seriously, enjoying all aspects of it and finding the fun in what I do. It wasn't an instant success because, as I mentioned many times, life can be messy and shit happens and when it does, it's easy to revert back to your default settings. So, with many failed attempts and setbacks, I'm finally managing to get it right. It will always be a work in progress, but life is so much more enjoyable.

We've all heard the phrase, 'Life is too short' and that's true, but life can be a long journey too—just ask any centurion. The thing is, whether life is too short or too long is irrelevant if you're not trying to be your best. Life to me is doing the things I like doing, in the places I like to be, with the people I like to be with, full stop! In my line of work, I've seen too many people unhappy about their career, relationships, body, looks etc and it's a waste of time and energy. If there is anything I would like people to take from reading this book or through meeting me, it's: MAKE LIFE FUN!

How do we make life fun?

First and foremost, keep it simple. I follow the ideas I outline in this book as my process of how to have fun. Having fun means that you are able to be grateful, connect and keep things simple. By applying these virtues to everything I do, I am able to find the significance in the activity.

Let me break that down:

- **Gratitude** is appreciating the good and bad and understanding that not everything is going to be fun but if you can find a reason, lesson or enjoyment in it, it's worth the effort.
- **Connection** is being and doing things I like with the people I care about and love. I know you can't always be with people you love and care about but whoever you're with, find something good about them, find a connection and do your best to make them feel good.
- **Simplicity** is finding the joy in the little things and not over complicating stuff.

There are many ways I try to do this and hopefully, I can enthuse you enough to maybe do the same. So, using the philosophy above, whether it's work or play, I try to find fun in what I do. There are times when it's bloody hard finding that fun, but I will always try my best to find something good or fun in what I do.

Below is a list of a few philosophies or methods I use to create fun in my world or to find some kind of enjoyment when things aren't so exciting. The point is, life isn't always going to be a ball of fun but if we can find the silver lining to make our world a little better, it may help make the world a better place.

I try to keep my approach simple and positive and try to hunt for the silver lining. It's not about always looking for the magical, it's about finding the magic in what you're looking at!

Work

Most of us need to work and with that, spend a lot of time there. If you like your job, that's great but if you don't, it can by shitty. I remember when I was in the trade, I used to clock-watch all day long just pining for the end of the day. I would break the day up into four quarters and think of it as a football game where I could talk myself through each quarter to make the day pass by, which was pretty soul destroying. Back then I let my negative mindset run my thinking because work was a chore and uninteresting. When I finally decided to do something about my predicament, I promised to myself that I'd never work in a job that had no significance for me.

Now, I'm grateful and very fortunate that I have a job I love and, most times, it's fun. It took some time to get to that stage. I remember the early days when I was doing about 4–5 different jobs to keep money coming in. One particular job that I disliked was selling sandwiches to local businesses. My role was walking into a business and selling the sandwiches which, for me, was hard work, slightly embarrassing and not much fun. To cut a long story short, I decided the only way I could get through this painful experience (I needed the money) was to drop my ego and just have some fun with it. My approach was to be engaging, interested and build a rapport with these people and in doing so, it changed the job completely. I ended up meeting some very interesting characters who not only made my job fun but bought the products too. The lesson I took from that experience was that my pride stopped me having fun and once I dropped my ego, the job was actually fun. I did it well and built some great connections for my business in the process. It was only a small change, but it worked.

Having a laugh

I like to laugh and hang with people who make me feel good. One of my favourite things is to hang with my brothers and just talk shit. We can be talking about anything and turn it into a funny story where we bang on about absolute rubbish and can laugh hysterically about it. It's sometimes so ridiculous yet quite often it brings tears to my eyes. It's a space where I feel so comfortable and can laugh freely, wholeheartedly, and it's fun. Comedy and humour are always a good way to have a laugh. Either watching a funny movie or show is a great way to have fun because sometimes we just need a laugh to take us away from the seriousness of the real world. Laughter is the best medicine. It draws people together in ways that trigger healthy physical and emotional changes in the body. Having a good laugh connects you to others, strengthens your immune system, boosts your mood, diminishes pain and reduces stress. And fortunately, I have seven brothers who can make me laugh enough to help me with that.

Try new things

Trying new things is fun. It enables you to expand your skills and learn. You don't have to make massive changes to do this. Keep it simple and find things that don't need a lot of preparation or props. Some of the things I've tried and continue to keep doing are: learning a new language, playing the guitar and drawing. These activities constantly challenge me so I'm continuously learning and finding new ways of becoming better at them.

I'll admit it, at times, they can get a little difficult but the learning and satisfaction I get from conquering a new phrase, song or technique has a genuine feel good factor about it and gives me the incentive to keep going. Doing new things helps me gain a better understanding of myself and enables me to explore my potential. We can easily get stuck in a routine or become stale because we fear change and end up living in a 'Groundhog Day' type of existence where nothing changes. I'm not suggesting you have to always be doing new things and challenging yourself but finding something that you can lose yourself in, is fun.

Music

The significance of music in my life is huge. I've always loved music ever since I was a little boy. I would listen to music and sing along to my favourite songs, pretending I was the lead singer or guitarist.

Music was my saviour, especially in my teens. It had such an impact on me and on the way I viewed the world. Bruce Springsteen (and the E Street band) was my go-to music. His lyrics resonated so deeply with me that it was like he was writing songs for and about me. At times I honestly believed that. There were many times I'd shut myself in a dark room and just listen to the songs because it allowed me to take my mind on a journey to another world and forget about life for a while.

Music is such an integral part of my life that it's become part of my everyday speak. I am constantly referring to a line of a song during a conversation. I believe there is a song for every occasion and if there isn't one, it's fun trying to find one. I use music in all aspects of life. You may have noticed the musical references throughout the book. I can't help it. Sorry! Music is a huge part of my makeup and has helped me through the good and the bad. It's a universal language that speaks all languages. Below is a poem I wrote that expresses what music means to me.

Music can lift your spirit,
ease your pain,
touch your heart
or bring the past back to life again.
It has a power that speaks where words often fail,
manipulates your emotions
but you're still in control.
It takes you on a journey
yet you never go away,
music is a therapy to be practiced every day.

How many times have you heard a song or piece of music that immediately triggers a memory? Music makes us nostalgic and we associate a song to a significant moment, a fond memory or experience in the past. I can recall so much of my past just by hearing a song. It immediately brings me straight back to a particular moment, experience, or event. Whether it was a school days crush, a major event or an emotional time, music has the ability to enable you to relive a feeling or a memory. Music has a healing power that produces biological changes in the body. It has the ability to lower your heart rate, decrease your blood pressure and reduce your stress levels. It's a powerful medicine for mood management. Whether it's to lift you up or calm you down, there's always a song that does the job. Music is also a wonderful connector, whether it's going to a concert with the masses or sitting with friends, it brings people together to share special moments and fun.

Travel

Travel is one of my greatest passions. I could write a book on this topic alone because there are so many benefits I receive from it. It allows me to connect with people from all around the world, experience different cultures and most of all, it's just good fun. I love exploring and immersing myself where I am. You know the saying, 'When in Rome do as the Romans do'? That couldn't be any more apt as a philosophy for when I travel. It allows me to be anonymous and keep things simple. The simple pleasure of strolling through a local market taking in the aromas, experiencing the atmosphere, or just sitting at a café people watching is awesome!

I love the fact that travel allows me to connect, share experience and have fun with people I've never met before. Like the time I was in Birmingham, Alabama on a work trip and I decided to go out for a drink on my own. I ended up meeting a group of locals and we had such an awesome night that developed into a friendship that we still maintain today. We just connected on a level that was simple, non-judgemental and I, at the time, was anonymous so there were no barriers or expectation on any of us and we all had fun. We had fun and that was what made it significant to me.

Not worrying about what others think

We can use so much unnecessary energy on worrying about what others think of us. In theory, it's easy to say, 'Don't worry about it' but we do! How many times have you stopped yourself from doing something because you felt silly or didn't want to embarrass yourself in front of others? This is a huge factor of why people don't try things or restrict themselves from having fun. I'm getting better at it but there was a time when I was so afraid to do things because I didn't want to look dumb or get ridiculed. I would either keep what I was doing to myself or if others were around, I wouldn't attempt it. In hindsight, I realised people don't care, they may say things to you but deep down they're don't really care.

This type of thinking is so restrictive and stops us from doing the things in life we'd like to do. For example, as I mentioned above, I love my music and, at times, am a bit partial to a sing song. I was with my cousins in Belfast, which can be a pretty tough place. My cousin set me up to sing karaoke in his local pub. I looked around the room and thought, 'No way! These guys look scary and if I'm terrible who knows what could happen?' I won't bore you with the finer details but eventually I got up to sing and decided to have fun with it. My singing wasn't the highlight, it was more the fun I put into it and during the song one of the guys who I earlier labelled as scary, gave me the thumbs up signal (which I must admit eased my concerns). After the performance, he actually took off his hat and walked around the room collecting coins from the crowd so I could buy myself some drinks for my effort. It was a hilarious moment that changed the whole atmosphere in the pub. The moral of the story: If I'd let the fear of how I looked or what people thought of me take over, I would never have experienced the fun we had that night. Yes, the chances of it being a shocker were high but when everyone picked up the fact, I was just having fun with singing in front of them, it filtered throughout the room and we all had a fantastic night.

Being adaptable

There will always be times when things go wrong or not according to your plans. Yes, it can be quite annoying but it's not about what happened, it's about how you react to what happens that's important. I'm sure we've all encountered a situation where we've been delayed, postponed or even stranded and thought; What the hell do I do now?' This experience can leave a bad taste in your mouth and your first reaction is to find someone or something to blame. Whereas, if you cool the jets a little and think about what you can do, most times it works itself out.

We love certainty but when our schedule or plans gets changed or interrupted, some people can become quite irrational and behave poorly. I can't believe how many times in my travels I've seen people react poorly and savagely lash out at the person on front desk because their schedule has been changed. The thing is, you can make as much noise and carry on all you like, but most times it's not going to change the situation. It's like watching a football game when a player argues with the umpire after giving away a free kick, hoping the decision gets reversed. It's a pointless exercise. The decision isn't going to change so just accept it and get on with the game.

To expect everything to run to schedule is a recipe for disappointment. Things will go wrong and most times, it'll be out of your control. To think otherwise, is kidding yourself. My philosophy when this happens is: accept it and find a way to adapt and make the situation the best you can. Many a travel plan has been changed or rescheduled and yes, it's annoying, but getting upset and abusive is a waste of time and energy. I try to adapt by finding a quiet spot to read, write, draw, people watch, or I sit in a café or a bar for a quiet drink or something to eat, and in doing so, I've had some great experiences and met some amazing people. I look at it as an opportunity to slow down and have some fun because there's always something you can do to adapt to the situation and pass the time away, no matter how long the delay.

Being adaptable can be fun. It helps reduce the stress and anxiety we create around wanting certainty. There have been many occasions where my plans have been changed through no fault of my own and, surprisingly, the situation has turned out for the better. Like during the COVID-19 pandemic, when my business was shut down for three months, I had to adapt to a new way to run my business. I went from face-to-face training to video link-ups, which at first was a little overwhelming. I didn't think it would work very well but I found it not only worked really well, I learned a lot about using technology and all the social media platforms. I could do pretty much the same type of training without even leaving home and it was fun. Not trying to control everything or expecting it to always go to plan makes life simpler and sometimes, when we you drop your expectations and just go with the flow, the journey can be more fun than the original plan.

Having fun doesn't have to be anything special, amazing or costly. It's about keeping life simple and looking for the silver lining in what you do. Life at times can be an absolute bitch, and how we choose to approach it is a choice. Life's not about what happens to you, it's about what you do with what happens to you and finding significance in it. You get to decide whether life is filled with complexity and seriousness or if you can keep it simple and fun. And by the way, whatever you decide, it doesn't matter. Personally, I believe if we all looked for the fun in what we do, we'd have more to be grateful for. We'd connect so much better and life would be simpler and that, to me, is finding significance in life.

Conclusion

Thank you for choosing this book. I really hope you enjoyed reading it and it resonated with you. The idea behind the book was to inspire you to believe you can be, do or create better without the pressure that tends to surround pursuing happiness and success. We all have the potential to achieve but sometimes the external pressure of comparison or insecurity gets in the way, so we let it hold us back. How often have we stopped ourselves from trying something new because we perceived it is all too hard or overwhelming and let fear and anxiety take control? As I have shown throughout the book, life is uncertain and at times deals us a shit hand but that shouldn't determine your outcome because life is a game to be played and how that game plays out, comes down to how much you're willing to try. Here's the thing: You'll never know how far you can go if you're not willing to try.

I'm passionate about finding significance in what we do. Some people have high expectations about how life should be and waste their valuable time worrying about what others think, comparing themselves to others, fearing failure, stressing or complaining about the unfairness of it all. Straight up, there's no such thing as fairness when we're talking about life. It's not what life owes us. It's what we owe to ourselves to make the best of what we have.

Life is a wonderful gift and it becomes even better when you can find significance in what you do. I believe that through finding significance in what we are doing, we start to understand and accept that we'll encounter adversity and failure, but we'll learn to be OK with that. Too many people spend most of their life chasing stuff, hoping it'll fill a void. When you see the significance in what you do, you start to understand the value of connection and why it's so important to survival. You develop gratitude, you stop comparing yourself to others and you live life according to your own rules.

Most of us want some form of success in life; however, we neglect to take the time to properly define what that success means to us. We believe we want grandeur yet when we strip back all the noise and bullshit around it, we realise all we really want is contentment and some fun. We tend to believe what popular psychology portrays as success, hoping for happiness or to be fixed. Yes, we're all a work in progress and somewhat broken but if we'd stop hoping and listen to our gut a bit more, we'd do things that align with our values and realise we're OK and don't need to be fixed.

Too many people waste life being miserable, hoping that someone or something will make them happy. It's time to slow down the urgency and busyness of life and start living it. Forget about chasing someone else's version of success and/or happiness or doing things to gain approval. Find what works for you and start following that. Try to reduce the expectation, stress, fear, and anxiety you put on yourself to achieve and accept that making a few mistakes along the way is part of the journey.

Life is often referred to as a race, which makes it sound like something you have to win. Life isn't about winners and losers. It's about finding what resonates with you and pursuing that. It's a wonderful opportunity to start writing your own unique story. We all have a story to tell and the best part is, how that story turns out is entirely up to you.

I believe success and happiness is achievable when approached the right way. Only you know what's right for you. How you live life is a personal thing and the sooner we eliminate the hype and noise around having to be somebody or something to be a success, and remove the emphasis on comparison and competition, the less intense our world will become. This winners and losers philosophy has made finding significance in your life more complicated than it needs to be. Somehow, we've become way too serious and made the pursuit of success/happiness so stressful, the enjoyment has gone, and we've forgotten how to have fun. What's success worth if it's overshadowed by pressure and anxiety? It's time to check your personal GPS and recalibrate your path. We can all achieve, find our own version of success, and be content with our lot in life if we simplify things, and have more fun through finding significance in what we do.

There's strength in simplicity and staying with that philosophy. If there's anything I hope you get from reading this book, it's to use the things that resonated for you to find significance in your life and then to share that philosophy with others to help them do the same. I wish you all the best in the story of you. Life is to be lived, to have fun and enjoy and it's doable when you find that significance in what you do, are grateful for what you have, accept who you are, and connect with others in a way that makes your part of the world a better place to live.

As much as life can be a bitch, keep it simple, stay true to your values and most of all, just keep trying!

Tread your path wisely. ☺